Twisted
Phone
Sex

Twisted Phone Sex:

Real Emails from Real Men

By

Mistress Candice

Tim Babiak of Exquisite Photography Austin,
Front cover photo and design, back cover photo.

Thanks to Larabe Freeware Fonts:
Blue Highway™, Teen™

Twisted Phone Sex: Real Emails from Real Men
By Mistress Candice
http://MistressCandice.com
2008 © by Mistress Candice
ISBN 978-0-578-00066-4

Dedicated to my mother for her
acceptance of my choices;
to my daughter for
her strength and patience;
to Tim for all his support and
all the photo shoots;
but mostly this book is dedicated
to all the women who chose
the road less traveled
and the men who opened
themselves up to us.

Table of Contents

Intro

This collection of Emails is only the tip of personal interaction between me and my clients. Like an iceberg the majority of the relationship is hidden from view. I present this book not only to entertain and amuse but to educate. Those who recognize themselves through someone else's words won't feel alone. Others may feel their fantasies small by comparison.

As entertaining as it is to look into someone else's imagination it should be equally insightful. For that reason I have left the text of the emails as unedited as possible. I leave it up to the reader to glean his or her own insights.

Twisted Phone Sex Mistress Candice

Not all the requests I have received over the years are included. Nor were all requests legal or granted. To avoid becoming boring or redundant, I selected this assortment based on their ability to represent, amuse and illustrate the rich fantasy life of men. I have never had a female customer, not that they don't exist, but every email in this book is from a man.

This book also contains a small glimpse into the daily life of a "Personal Entertainment Specialist." Through these email's readers will be able to watch my evolution from Web cam girl, to phone sex operator, to dominatrix and then almost solely an erotic hypnotist. Maybe it is a sign of the times or an indication of bigger things to come but erotic hypnosis seems to be more popular and more lucrative than performing naked before a web cam or talking dirty to someone's frustrated husband on his lunch hour.

Erotic hypnosis is different things to different people but in actuality it is exactly as it sounds; conventional hypnosis with an erotic twist. Initially I discuss with the prospective subject what they would like to experience or what they hope to gain. Once I have a relatively reasonable understanding, I use a progressive relaxation induction to relax them, which takes about 15 to 20 minutes. Once hypnotized, I create the circumstances for them to experience what they requested: a tailor-made fantasy with an anonymous woman. On the average, a session lasts approximately 45 minutes. I can't say everyone is hypnotized, but it doesn't matter as long as they enjoy the experience.

So in a way, this book shows the every day guy and how he spends his time when he steals a few brief moments for himself. While reading keep in mind these men are from every walk of life. Rich and poor, married and single. They are your brother, your father, your son, your spouse and even the person sitting next to you as you read this. Perhaps, someday, it could easily be you. It is my greatest hope that my readers will come to understand the importance of tolerance and reserving judgment.

"The noblest pleasure of all is the joy of understanding."

– Leonardo diVinci

Chapter One

Costumes and Props

On a Webcam or when using the phone only, the visual showing a hot woman, even if it's only in a man's mind, can be made even more erotic through props and costumes. What she is wearing and what she is playing with become part of the attraction. The range and variety of items of apparel and accessories, objects, gadgets, or toys are as limitless as a man's imagination.

Twisted Phone Sex

Mistress Candice

Do you have any BIG toys, like the size of a baseball bat?

Hi there, I would love to set up a phone/cam session I love sexy lingered and you come home to find me in your room and I am at your dresser with your lingerie drawer open and I am dressed up in a bra and panty set jerking off looking at a picture of you I look up and see you let me know who catches me is it mommy coming home from work in her suit and sexy lingerie underneath or is it sis coming home from school in her cute little pigtails in her new bra and panty set under let me know

I was curious what you are wearing! Hopefully something with stockings

Can you dress you like a little punk chick for me? I'll call in about 5 min

Twisted Phone Sex

Hi,

Do you have any naughty nurse costumes with stockings?

Will you use the heel of your shoe to fuck yourself with?

Hi you.... I'm in need of your services, as well as the services of your bountiful tits. I want you in a TIGHT outfit.

You have great reviews and look gorgeous. I wonder if you ever dressed in a knee length skirt, with stockings and garter belt underneath and a slip. On top have a camisole top or sexy bra with a blouse. I love when women dress conservatively, but have very sexy lingerie on underneath and tease.

Twisted Phone Sex Mistress Candice

Do you have any outfits / uniforms for your shows?

Do you have any metallic dresses and clear platform heels? I like women to dress up like androids to support the role play.

Would you wear stockings and a garter belt & play with yourself while we talk? If so I will call you this afternoon at 5:30 PST

Hi,

I see you have toys listed but will you use regular household items. A brush handle or plunger, stuff like that?

Do you ever sell your panties? I like them used I want to smell you on them. I will pay for a show too so I can see you in them. Thanks.

Do you have Boots or stockings for a show?

Do you have five inch heels? Will you suck on the heel like it's a dick for me?

I love your pictures; do you have some nice black stockings that you could wear for me on cam? If so I will be calling in a second.

I love nylons. Do you have any tan nylons with the toes and the control tops? Will you sell them to me?

Hey,

Do you have any anal toys?

Twisted Phone Sex Mistress Candice

Do you have any shiny latex outfits? I like the little shorts or mini skirts.

I'm really into hot bikini babes wearing cowboy hats and riding me!!!! Are you interested?

A woman in a tight fitting pair of jeans and a low cut top make me want to burst through my pants!!!!!!!!!!!!!!!!! Boots are a plus. I want to see you dance for me like we were at a club and then you just start ripping your clothes off because you get so into it. And I like know you have to keep them on but you ignore me. Are You up for it?

What kind of panties do you have? I like them really lacy and I prefer red or black.

My cock is aching to see you on cam in a black latex Dom outfit and fur ordering me to worship your ass! I think its time to play with you :) Can I come say hi and we can start a show? Oh before I go could you please wear leather or latex I would like to be humiliated and tortured just a little too

Do you ever seduce a new thrall with glittering finery and crystals nestled perfectly between your perfect breasts?

Do you have any lacy lingerie to wear? Something really sexy and seductive? I want you to be my best friend's mom and seduce me when I come over looking for him.

Baby I miss you...

Twisted Phone Sex Mistress Candice

Any sheer pantyhose yet?

I would love to see you in a slip, stockings, knee length skirt and blouse. You have excellent reviews and would love to play with you. Let me know if you have that.

This is so frustrating. Your picture in white silk and those white stockings and clear high heels is so sexy. There is a need like a hunger inside me to hear your voice. I really hope we can get to talk soon.

I love your blood red nails, I love you. I have never loved another woman the way I love you, all I can think about is your delicious sexy blood red nails.

Twisted Phone Sex

Hello. I am curious if you would be interested in the following: I would like to send you some pictures and have you give me an honest assessment of my size. When I get your opinion on my size, I will call and during the cam/call, I would like to chat about my size, what you think, and have you ask questions and comment. Also, I would love to hear about the smallest and biggest you have seen and you have had sex with. During the call, I would love for us to mutually masturbate together as we discuss this. Do you have any sheer stockings you can wear and can you keep the cam back so that I can see you from your stocking feet to your face? Finally, I can masturbate either naked or with a pair of Victoria's Secret Seamless pantyhose on. Whichever you prefer is great. Thanks.

Hi, I have not spoken with you before but I would love to see you in white stockings, see your painted toes, and have you play with my ass. I am your 18 year old neighbor boy you invite over.

Twisted Phone Sex

Mistress Candice

Hi!

Just saw that you were online and had to tell you that you have incredible legs! I am a TRUE leg man, and yours are perfect! Do you have any silky, sheer stockings you could show me? I'd love to see those perfect legs up close in a pair of white or black nylons and your feet in some spiky heels. Please let me know. Hope to see you and chat with you soon!

When might you be available in your gloves and boots for cam?

I saw the picture where you have red nails and fur coat, and I think that is very sexy. Do you usually dress like that every time when you're on? Thinking about calling you today what is your msn and do u have thigh high stockings?

Do you have any full pantyhose today for a show like this?

Twisted Phone Sex

Long time no chat....
Still hoping to see you on cam in a pair of sheer
pantyhose preferably black or dark tan...
Have you had a chance to get any yet? Let me
know when you get a minute to reply...

Do you have any half slips?

Dear Goddess,

I am interested in a call with you tonight. Do you have a short skirt and a tight tube top u can wear?

Hi, was wondering if u could wear the red top and that cute red skirt u have on you are site. With the neck chocker too I think that is hot! Thanks

Twisted Phone Sex

Mistress Candice

I would love to see you in tight jeans and sexy heels, pictures or videos

Avail for show with thigh high boots or stockings???

Do you have a latex mini skirt? Red or black will be fine

Do you have a nurse's costume or a cop costume you can wear for a show?

Do you Have platform shoes? I want you to pretend you are squishing a bug with them.

Do you have any tan or black nylons? The full nylons not stockings.

I get really HOT HOT HOT for full bottom panties, no thongs. I just want you to model all that you have for me and then when I find a pair I like I want you to pose like a mannequin but I get to pose you.

Do you have any red pumps you can wear during session or maybe some with metal heels?

I know this sounds weird but do you have a snorkel and mask? I just want you to get real close to the camera with your face with those on. I hope you don't think that is too weird.

Twisted Phone Sex Mistress Candice

Do you have and long cigarette holders? I love a classy woman who smokes while tapping her nails and looking straight at me.

Do you have any high heeled open toed shoes? Do you have a pedicure? What color are your toenails?

I love glittery jewelry on a woman. The kind you have on your pictures. Do you wear them for live shows? I would love to come in and see.

Does your cheerleader costume come with pom poms?

Can you wear full bottom white panties underneath your school girl skirt?

Do you have any see through tops you can wear? Maybe get them wet?

Do you have a pair of really high pumps that you could pretend you were stepping on my balls with?

Do you do clothing requests? You are so hot and I have wanted a show with you forever!!!!

Do you have a bunch of skin tight mini dresses you can try on for me? I just want you to tease me as you change never showing me anything. Except maybe once in a while your strap will fall and your breast will show but you cover it up really fast like it was an accident and you are embarrassed.

Twisted Phone Sex

Mistress Candice

Hi Miss,

Do you have any strap ons? I love to see a woman wearing a big dick.

Do you have a slutty secretary outfit handy??

Chapter Two

Humiliate Me

The most common theme in domination is humiliation. Humiliation has become so common; I refer to it as "mainstream." Not a day goes by where I haven't had at least one request to humiliate someone in one way or another. It is more popular and more lucrative than straight sex and it can be more interesting.

Twisted Phone Sex

Mistress Candice

Mistress: Do you offer custom pictures for sale via paid mail? *blushing* Thank you for considering... ok, here goes (if I don't chicken out). I would love to be humiliated by you in a few pictures... *blush*... I could send you a picture of me (naked) that you could print and hold up to the camera and laugh and point at (or flip me off)? Gulp! You have a mischievous look, I think you would make an awesome teasing humiliator and would love a few of you teasing me in this way. Let me know what you think... I can't believe I am asking you this! Devoted, slave

Mistress: Thank You for the pictures... Oh my god, I am blushing deep red but my heart is racing as well! Thank You... they are wonderful! I was able to download without a problem. Looking forward to future encounters also... *gulp* devoted, slave

Twisted Phone Sex

Hello Mistress,

I am into forced intoxication (the more I drink the more I will do), forced Fem, cross dressing, public humiliation, and some Cock and Ball Torture. I am in a hotel room and will drink and dress at your command. I also have a webcam so you can see that I drink and do as you command. My instant message id is: XXXX. Are you into these things?

You're Servant,

Dear Mistress... what wish list gifts do you want most... would you like a gas card with your name on it as my treat... I pay the monthly bills... punish me

Can I be your online slave? I can tribute via paid e mails

I would love to worship you through Tribute

Twisted Phone Sex

Mistress Candice

Hi there, I find women very attractive and I am not gay. I think you are really beautiful. I am a loser with a little dick, only 4" long when hard. I'm seeking a woman to encourage me to jerk off regularly and then eat my own cum. I also have a 6" pink rubber dildo that I would suck on for you. If you like, I'll dip the dildo in warm lemonade before I suck on it. I have no interest in anal sex or Cock and Ball Torture. But I would love to kiss and lick your ass. If this appeals to you, I NEED you to watch me on cam doing this. I would most likely call on the weekend but I can't predict when the urge will strike.

I'd love to get a show where you humiliate me and make me say things like how much I love to suck cock and service men. Make me say how I love you not my girlfriend and how much I need you. Let me know if this is ok

Twisted Phone Sex

I have a tiny dick and I am shy and embarrassed. I want to call so you can make fun of it but I don't want to say anything or talk. Can we do that?

I would love for you to have me secured to a bed or couch and you are queening me, then you decide to force me to eat your sweet beautiful pussy clean after your boy friend secretly fucks you quietly in another room...

Would you like to make me cum and spread it on my face and eat it? I don't have a webcam but I could send you pictures. What would you do with the pictures? If you post them can you take them down after a week or two?

May I please continue my slavery to you and your super beautiful feet? I would love to bathe in your foot sweat and be humiliated and denied by you

Twisted Phone Sex

Mistress Candice

I would love for you to seduce me, tie me up....
then secretly give me cream pie surprise while you
girlfriend and her bf watch so they can learn how
to do that..

**I was told by my mistress to find a
submissive girl and be her bitch. So I
desire to humiliate myself for your
amusement. If you desire for me to kiss
your feet I shall. I will do anything you
ask to amuse you even if you tell me to
stick my head in the toilet.**

Twisted Phone Sex

Hi Mistress! I would love the opportunity to be your obedient foot slave :) It would be my honor to submit to you in any way you deem appropriate. Public humiliation, tease and denial, tickle torture, and generally being abused are some of my favorites.

Hello Mistress, are you online today... I so missed you... please I want so much more from you... I want you to take over my life... please... wow. I loved the picture of you with the dog collar/... it drove me wild....please put it around my neck

I've only talked to a few here, and haven't really been satisfied. Then again I'm also kind of embarrassed to say what I really want. But after reading your info, seeing your gorgeous face, and seeing your high ratings, I thought I'd give you a shot. (I'm about to give up on this whole thing too) I really want a Mistress to control me. Not just on the phone, but with rules from day to day. Like chastity and

Twisted Phone Sex

denial or when to call. Also I am little embarrassed about this but I want to wear women's lingerie. I am also big into humiliation/degradation. And the list can go on, but I don't want to bore you with all this--I'm sure someone as beautiful as you is so busy! So if you could reply at all I would be so happy!*huge grin* I'm up for things like premature ejaculation because they are so dysfunctional but things like panty-sniffing, compulsive masturbation or even things like needing to suck my thumb to go to sleep are all on the table. Really it's anything that makes me less a man, less desirable in bed or just... less ;)

Please can I be your cam2cam slave Goddess? I have webcam and sum toys and sissy clothes, is there anything in particular I will need Princess?

Just got a webcam would you like to humiliate me and watch and also make me eat my cum?

Twisted Phone Sex

Hey can you sit topless on cam and laugh at me while I jack off while telling me I'm a loser that has to pay?

Mistress, you look so amazing. I have a big breast fetish and I'm worried that if I call you will entrance me and make me addicted to you. But I keep coming back to your photos.....How can I escape from this?

Would you settle for a teeny weenie?

I was wanting a chance to cuck-serve you this evening.

Twisted Phone Sex   Mistress Candice

I was wondering if you wanted to make me your slave boy! lol   It would be great to be controlled by you. You could hypnotize or brainwash me into becoming your slave and give me stroking instructions, keep me on the line for as long or as short as you like. You could force me to pay you $100 whenever you make me cum and to call you back and do it all over again whenever you send me an IM telling me to call. Maybe you could even be so devious as to force me to watch porn all day, that way you can do the most damage to my wallet. I don't check email that much, but if you want immediate servitude, send me an internet message.

Would love to be your adoring sub meat puppet!

Twisted Phone Sex

I would so love to be tied up by you again and feel your soft sexy pussy on my face... before you get nasty and make me rim your sweet asshole moments after your lover exploded in your pussy, and he is just sitting back watching you laugh at me as you wait for the cum to drip down in your crack and in my mouth... urging me to be a good little puppy for you.. Ahhhh...

Hi Mistress, a list of my total weaknesses, Verbal abuse, tease and denial, ass tease and worship, bitchy attitude, addiction, laughed at, spit on, Hypnosis, brainwash. Thank you. I will call when I am done.

I can't get over how incredible you are. I listened to Control 101 and Devotion 102 and it's taking every bit of willpower I have left to stay off here. I still am compelled to listen to your perfect, seductive, so perfect powerful voice almost every night. I have a feeling it's only a matter of time before I'll be breaking down and begging you to let me be your bitch.

Mmmm you wouldn't fuck me with a strap on?

Twisted Phone Sex

Thank you baby...right now, there is another Man playing with that cleavage and your soooo sexy bra...and that makes me hot....imagining what he is doing to you and you to him....I get so hard when I think of how his hands are wandering around on you sexy body....

Mistress,
I feel like your little toy. I wish I was there doing whatever it is you want! I must be careful, I feel myself slipping into your beautiful clutches. Your recordings are starting to have a serious effect on me and my little buddy. ;)

Twisted Phone Sex

I don't want to eat my cum yet I know I have to obey you and make you happy. I am trying to not listen to this yet I have to I no I can't resist You, I love obeying you

I would love to worship/cuck-serve you. I would gladly do it RL or on-line, I just don't ever catch you on....(=

I appreciate the invitation and love the picture, thank You. I love chastity and cuckolding and would like to talk to you sometime.

Twisted Phone Sex

If only you enjoyed acting like a arrogant neighbor as you enjoyed setting up my initiation - you seduce and trap me in bondage and force-feed me my first cream pie without me realizing it at all and with your friend(s) quietly observing and encouraging you to complete my indoctrination as you rub it all over my face and in my mouth, until you get me to say I love the taste and are sure I can handle the taste without realizing what it really is! Then while sitting on my face covering my eyes, you carefully and quietly guide your lover into your sweet ass or pussy as you ensure that all of your hidden friends can see you mock me and have sex over my face - exploding again and again as you give me kudos for having such a fantastic tongue and making me think you are also playing with a dildo over my face or maybe your girlfriend is? You moan as you fill my mouth with your sweet love juices until you finally let him explode inside you and above your Venus to set up my public degradation as you let your friends watch how you make it all slowly drip into my throat... until you are clean... making me worship your ass and clean that as well... such a sweet creamy chocolate pie that you teach me to eat as well... making me your cream pie eating and cleaning slave... I would be such a loyal puppy for you if you kept me as your own!

I'm sorry mistress I got cut off, I promise next will do long session just got to pick the right time when no roommates are around, maybe u hypnotize me and shove that cock in me, love that pick by the way thank you. But I can't wait to have u in me, what is the hypno like with strap on play?

Twisted Phone Sex

Any chance you're into the more extreme humiliation? I'm a pretty crappy lover and I have a history of it, I first masturbated with my face in my mothers panties and it just went downhill, I lost my virginity in 3 strokes, my ex-wife told me that she used to fake orgasms because she couldn't feel me and I would fall out. Even my current fiancée (who is a traditional virgin and only gives me blowjobs so far) is surprised when I cum quickly in her mouth, usually saying "Wow, you came so quickly!" or something. The only way I even get it hard (except when I'm playing with it, which I do 2-3 times a day if I can) when I'm with a girl is to imagine something more fitting the size of the cock. Sound like something you'd like?

Twisted Phone Sex

Mistress Candice

Goddess, I am sooo in need of hearing you laugh and call me names, please pleases please be a major bitch to me and drain my balls, its so not fair how addicted u make me, kneeling, please be a major bitch and laugh your ass of calling me names(verbal abuse) taking all my cum away as I shoot in my face Oh my god I am so in love with your cleavage shots, your busy and I am on my knees waiting for you to ruin my Sunday and my date, if I cum I wont be able to screw a little later, and you would have controlled my day and date, you make me worthless, I am a dumb ass for you mistress,

Um... I... maybe, if it's ok to ask... can I even ask? Can I even ask what my life would be like if I do totally give in? I mean, right now it seems like I fight it constantly every second that I'm home or that I'm on-line... can I ask what my life would be like owned by you, totally brainwashed and.. Well, to live as your bitch day in and day out?

38

Kneeling, I just got back from date, I think she knows I have a little penis, now I am forced to call u when I need to cum, help, it's so not fair that I have to pay per minute to touch my little pathetic thing, are you on now? Its 9pm.

Hi goddess, I already made a mess twice today thinking about how you verbally abused me and I lost that chick do to not getting excited by her, u are the only one who can make me cum, why do u do this?? I am so in love with your cruel addicting attitude, kneeling, please be a bitch to me today, I need to cum 3 times total, and do you have the power to make me shoot in my face

Twisted Phone Sex

Goddess, u killed me yesterday when u made me cum, I cant get laid now, your busy now but I am home tonight, I am slowly going into dept, this phone line will ruin me, please hook me and take over my life, I love the laugh and hearing u make fun of me, that cleavage and ass are unreal, kneeling

Hi goddess, are you going to take all my cum away so I can't get laid today?? u are so mean to me, my little cock craves your verbal abuse and name calling along with that evil laugh, why do I crave you so much? Help your weakened slave,

Twisted Phone Sex

I'm in a naughty mood... I'd love to be your bitch tonight. I wonder what dirty things you'd make me do... It's too bad... I normally like to be on top and have a sexy girl like you do what I want. Tonight I'd be your whore. Sorry we couldn't connect today.

Twisted Phone Sex   Mistress Candice

I am very shy so I thought id email first. I have a fantasy of being dominated made to wear woman's clothes etc I've never acted on it but I saw your ad and thought maybe you could help. Hope to hear from you soon kneeling, hi goddess, my mind is flattered and need to hear u laugh, call me names, swear at me, verbally abusing me, telling me my life is over and I will not get laid again, the only time I can cum is when you make me, I so need to cum today,. I love your voice and am glad u have molded me to be your dumb ass cum pig, please laugh and call me names forcing my dumb cum out, you rule,

You are very fine!! Do you like to play blackmail games?

Twisted Phone Sex

Goddess, you have taken over my life, kneeling help my pathetic existence. I love hearing u degrade and laugh at me, your words are so powerful, and the only time I can come is when I hear you

Hi goddess, in such need of your power and abuse. Please drain my weak balls

Hi goddess, I cant get interested in the girls who come over to screw, my little penis wont grow unless I see your pictures and hear u humiliate me, u have me by the balls, god help me. Are you going to take all my cum away again?? I have a hottie coming over later, if you drain me I won't be able to get laid and she will never come back which I means I have to call u always to cum, so not fair goddess, help...

Twisted Phone Sex

Mistress Candice

Hi - I have an odd castration fantasy I'd love to play with you. Basically you are my wife, and I know you go out with other guys. I say it's ok, but you think it makes me sad, and you hate coming home to my little erection all the time. So you decide to "fix" it by removing my balls! You have to talk me into it and get me to agree - no pain, surgically done, by you. Just take off the nuts - what do you think??

Help, my little weenie needs to spurt all over my stomach, do u have to power tonight goddess? I'm sooo dumb and get so excited when you drain my balls laughing at calling me names. What do I do?

Hey can you sit topless on cam and laugh at me while I jack off while telling me I'm a loser that has to pay?

Yes yes been dying to hear u, your soo precious, please be a laughing mean bitch and take my come away, please??? Your soo awesome, my brain and mind is addicted

OOOOHHHHHH, I did have fun and I did meet that guy at P10 and took him the men's room and sucked him off in the stall it was awesome...I almost came with out even touching myself, just from having his cock in my mouth. I will talk again to you soon.

Twisted Phone Sex

Mistress Candice

I have a new fantasy that I'm a little shy about and I wonder if you could help. But it may not be for everyone... Ok here goes nothing: I have only been with women, I just turned 30 (yikes) and have had my fair share of hot girls in my day. But recently I've become curious about what it would be like to be with a man and in particular to be with a man who is well endowed, hence my question to you. I saw this porno where this girl was getting fucked by a guy who was really big and she seemed to be having the time of her life - not porn faking but genuinely enjoying herself in a big way (pun unintended hee hee). Something strange happened to me, I thought "why should I be left out?" and then second thought - even more confusing and strangely erotic for me was the thought of wanting to switch places with the girl in the video. It's the first time I've ever wanted to be a girl getting fucked by a man! I've been so curious that I went out and bought a toy and I tried it and enjoyed it but I felt a little awkward doing it by myself. It was a smaller toy and while it was an interesting experience it was not fulfilling the fantasy. Yesterday the bigger toy that I ordered arrived in the mail and I am very curious to try it.

Twisted Phone Sex

I'd love to meet u at a "safe" place, chat, buy u a drink like I was putting the moves on you, but then u put something in my drink or food, then after the right amount of time, invite me up to your suite.. As I wake up in the dark, I hear you chatting with friends, but notice I am unable move, then hear you walking towards me and see the light come in as you raise the lid on the box (use your imagination here) and say hi and inform me that I am the guest of honor at a private contest. Judging who has the best all around ass and pussy. As you laugh and sit down on my face, then press a button that raises my head up and pushed my face deep into your ass hole. As I struggle to breath and please you. Then I notice the protective black linings have been removed from outside the exterior walls of the box my head is in, revealing a clear and transparent plexi-glass construction, which must be upon an elevate throne type structure because I can see at eye level the faces of your nasty minded girl friends looking at my trapped face as you press the button again sealing my face in your ass. Now commanding me to taste your superior ass cream... laughing at me... How nasty could you be while using my face/mouth if you had it trapped in this type of box? Or just tied up? I can imagine some nasty acts with a room full of sexy girls. Maybe one

Twisted Phone Sex

Still suffering, oh my god your unreal, I am home tonight, are you going to take my cum away? Why do you get so excited when you laugh call me names and be mean to me? I can't keep a girl cause only you get me excited, kneeling, its 9pm eastern time, what time are you on until mistress? Please be a bitch.

Hello Mistress Its your devoted young slave that aches and begs to serve you in real life. This sucks I finally have free time to serve you but it appears I will have to wait as you are busy w/ other more important queen stuff. So I guess I all go back to my cage in your garden and listen to the mp3s and wait for my Goddess another day. Crawling away now Bye for now my sweet Goddess/Owner.

What time today I have so much to share about a new sex drive all the cumming one can want even with out touching it. All guys should know this....I wore wife's panties today and I haven't played or cum in them in a while. Hope you can come on early

masturbate with me? Will you also finger and dildo during our call? I hope this is something you would find enjoyable and that you will give me an honest opinion of my penis size and be sincere and truthful in your comments. Thanks very much

Hi, will u call me names and swear at me laughing your ass of on how addicted and how ruined u will make me down the road, verbal abuse, cleavage tease, ass worship, ass tease, g-string, and a bitchy attitude will get me forever, oh yeah also talking about suckering my $$ away, making me a broke loser

Twisted Phone Sex   Mistress Candice

You around today? Got any ideas for adding a VERY humiliating real trigger session today? Maybe something involving me in **pink panties** that get accidentally exposed in public (zipper lowered at the worst moment), and slow embarrassing loss of my clothes...and finally **totally RED faced** as I find myself actually on my knees cock sucking...a telltale boner dripping but not relieved...yet.

Your ideas really turned me on. Would you please consider making an mp3 for me? I'm married, intelligent, and straight but I just can't stop thinking these thoughts. About what you would say to me as you make me stand before you, so humiliated. How you are going to tell my wife. How you're going to introduce her to things. I'd like you also to make an mp3 for my wife.

She's curious about this lifestyle and we've talked about hypnosis to help calm her and relax her with these ideas. Please email me at xxxxx.com. I'm kind of new to this and it's all overwhelming

Twisted Phone Sex

Hello Goddess:

Love to become your slut pig I am located in Chicago, Austin, and visit Glory holes, bathhouses, truck stops and fag theaters I keep getting fatter, sleazier now and Drink gin, vodka, rum and sniff poppers I swallow black dicks and cum loads when I am told And take it up the ass Do you think im becoming an ugly faggot pig? Fantasy pig

My wife just had me put my butt plug in so I am ready for tonight I want to call and you force me to masturbate and cum with my wife in the next room. It would turn me on for you to make fun of her and humiliate her, while you make me worship you. I would like a task before I call, so I will be ready. Shall I call Goddess? If I said I wanted you to harshly and dramatically transform daddy into an unrecognizable and permanent slut whore, you'd say.

Twisted Phone Sex

Mistress Candice

can u take over my little mind again and talk about the asses and power you have over my little weenie, the last calls were awesome, please use my weakness to get me addicted, I think u have all them, I need to lose control all over me, I love when u get into my head and do the ass talk and verbal abuse, please see my fetishes,

Twisted Phone Sex

I will need your help and full control to help make this worse for me. My GF isn't kinky enough and I'm too scared now that my balls are full LOL. I'm thinking this has several elements...first when she comes over tonight before I pick/remove another marble we need a way to make the likelihood of a green marble go down (prolonged chastity will make me even more desperate and willing to do ANYTHING). My GF will not suggest that...so somehow taking the 30 blue marbles in the sack and getting way up (there's 60 more) is what needs to happen. It hurts to even type that sentence so don't look for help from me LOL Watching more marbles being slowly added makes my nuts tingle...Second...somehow she needs to get the idea that choosing EXTRA (more than the allotted one) marbles on a given night should cum at a price....and that's where the fun can start. I already wear panties when I pick a marble... Maybe offer more and more...as long as it's very humiliating and she's in charge...Third, if she starts to complain about being horny (she has in past games but not yet) that's an opportunity to get cuckolded IRL...as long as I can watch dressed in something embarrassing. That can be suggested...remember she doesn't tend to think of this stuff so it has to be suggested or it doesn't happen. Add anything else you think would make it deliciously evil and prolong my agony a LOOONG time...!?!?!

Twisted Phone Sex

Mistress Candice

I recently saw your listing and would love to set a phone/webcam session up. I am 28 and particularly like all types of kinky sex. My main (but not only) interest is domination particularly intense CBT, humiliation, tease/denial and so on. I also really like to be made to have strange/painful/humiliating orgasms. Perhaps you have some good ideas of things we could do? I would love something completely new or unexpected as sometime it can be quite boring and predictable to do the same things! Also, I adore sexy outfits particularly short skirts, stockings, fetish wear, spiked heels etc. I love variety and am very visually stimulated.

Twisted Phone Sex

id love to be staring at your sweet ass on my knees...
looking at your beautiful ass and wondering if you had
just fucked someone... as I feel you tug on a leash that is
attached to a collar that I was wearing... pulling my
face and mouth into your sweet ass and pussy...
surprised as I feel your hand grab my hair and your bf's
hands pushing the back of my head into your perfectly
fucked pussy... both of you laughing at me as you force
me to clean you out and wipe yourself on my face...
telling me that you will tell my mom/wife/boss if I don't
keep doing this for both of you at least once per week...
or when you call me over for a clean up... trapping me
into being your little slave mouth boy toy...

I would love for you to seduce me, tie me up.... then secretly
give me cream pie surprise while you gf and her bf watch..
to learn how to do that..

Twisted Phone Sex

Mistress Candice

Hi, I was wondering and hoping if you could enjoy sensually luring me (your ex-bf that you dumped months ago) via some of your best conniving and manipulating techniques into sensual bondage. You know I have a weakness for eating your hot sweet pussy and ass and you promise me a night I would never forget. After I am tied up by you your current bf (possibly black) shows up and you seductively and wickedly climb on top of my face and let him fuck you until he explodes all inside you. Your knew bf enjoys pulling out of your beautiful pussy and pushing mf face deep into your pussy as he laughs and you join in. Of course, you smother me afterwards with your warm wet pussy and ass and make me lick you clean, two or three times. Informing me of how much better of a lover he is and that you had decided to make me your little cream pie slave and I was just going to get use to cleaning up his mess, or your next lover(s), or even your special girlfriends and other couples. Now you also know that I still really love you and you whisper to me that I would do this for you if I really wanted to get back together and you promise

56

that you would take me back at some point in the future, laughing privately with your girlfriends as they all know that you will only take me back as a private cream pie eating cuckold slave...

Hello Candice. I absolutely love your pics and would love to do a cam/call with you. I am looking to do a cam/call with someone who is sincere and honest with me about the size of my penis. I don't want to hear that it is the smallest penis ever if it isn't, I don't want to hear that it is average or big if it isn't. I would love to do a call with someone who will give me an honest assessment, which is what I hope you will do (your page looks like you would be honest and I am really looking for this). If you would be interested, I can send three pics, one of me soft, one of me hard from the front and one of me hard from the side. I would love to hear what you think of my penis before our call, and also if you think sex with a penis my size would be enjoyable or unsatisfying. For our call, I would love to mutually masturbate while we discuss my penis, its size, and how fulfilling or unfulfilling it would be to have sex with something of that size. I would also love to hear about the smallest and largest penises you have had sex with and what each felt like, and also rate my penis on a scale of 1 to 10, one being the smallest penis and 10 being the largest penis. You may ask me whatever you feel like during

the call, depending upon what you think of my penis and how you feel about talking with me. You may ask me questions or make me says things, again, depending upon what you feel like. I can send you my yahoo or eyeball cam as well if you would like to watch. I won't show my face and my cam is slow, but it will give you a visual if you enjoy this. My yahoo and eyeball id is trapley321. Also, would you be willing to wear sheer stockings and some sheer or lacy lingerie and keep the cam back so that I can see your from your stocking feet to your face while you

Hi Mistress Candice! i would love the opportunity to be Your obedient foot slave :) It would be my honor to submit to You in any way You deem appropriate. Public humiliation, tease and denial, tickle torture, and generally being abused are some of my favorites.

Would you like to make me cum and spread it on my face and eat it? i don't have a webcam but i could send you pics.? You could sell if off your site for a week or to or just sell it as a payment request off your site to show people i am your whore if you like.

Hi,

I saw your listing and would love to have a session with you. I've been hypnotized before on the phone and I love it. I have a small cock (a little less than 5 inches and really skinny) and I would love to be hypnotized and humiliated about it. I'm also really into being made to be a premature ejaculator or making it harder to get or keep an erection even if I do end up with a girl. Something that has worked well in the past has been focusing on how good it feels to slip inside a woman - how blissful those first few seconds are, how easy and natural it is to orgasm just as soon as I enter a woman. How my short cock can't please her anyways so I might as well just cum immediately. Just a thought - I'll be happy with whatever you want to do! You can be as humiliating or degrading as you want and I'm open to any post-hypnotic suggestions or new humiliating behaviors' (private ones like panty-sniffing or more public ones are both ok). Is that something that might appeal to you?

I have a tiny dick though and I am shy and embarrassed.

I was told by my mistress to find a submissive girl and be her bitch. So I desire to humiliate myself for your amusement. If you desire for me to kiss your feet I shall. I will do anything you ask to amuse you even if you tell me to stick my head in the toilet.

Mistress is there something humiliating you would like to make me do for you. I don't have a webcam but I do have a digital camera that I could take pics with for you. What would you do with the pics mistress? By the way I don't have any toys or female clothes, but if you can think of something no matter what it is I will do it.

I'd love to get a show where you humiliate me and make me say things like how much I love to suck cock and service men. Make me say how I love you not my gf and how much I need you. Let me know if this is ok

Twisted Phone Sex

Mistress Candice

Hi goddess, kneeling, I was wondering if I can call and hear you be a major bitch calling me names and laughing at me little weenie, I crave verbal abuse, being laughed at, ass tease, ass worship, brainwashing, yelled at, and forced to come in my mouth as you laugh as I get addicted, please make this call so addicting

I want to be feminized and I need your help...I think it is time to go the store and have you on speaker. What will you have me buy today so that everyone can hear you? I need the humiliation. Would you make me over to the extreme with heavy makeup and multiple piercing.

Maybe tattoos. I want to look ridiculous and like a trashy cocksucker. I want you to make it so I can never be a man again. Then after I work for you, will you bind me, take photos you can send to my wife and family and then lock me in a crate and leave me in an abandoned warehouse.

Twisted Phone Sex

Mistress Candice

Chapter Three
Hypnosis Requests

Whether they are looking to be hypnotized, or they simply want to role-play being hypnotized, the sky is the limit.   For no matter what the request, the theme is simple "make me do it". This growing field in the sex industry is virtually in its infancy, but it is an expanding market, growing by leaps and bounds.   When given the choice between viewing me through a web cam or closing their eyes and living the fantasy through hypnosis, 9 out of 10 times they chose hypnosis even if they have never been hypnotized before.

Twisted Phone Sex Mistress Candice

I have been hypnotized before. I used to worship and belong to another Mistress. I don't know if you know who she is. She just doesn't have enough time for slaves, she never communicates directly. She makes you go through 6 weeks of mp3 training (which I did) and conditioning. So I have been conditioned. I am really into hypnosis, financial domination, worship, foot worship, hand worship. I love your jewelry by the way. It is very hypnotic along with your amazing hands. Let me know what you think, I don't have my cam right now sorry. But I do have lots of pictures. I have to shower real quick be back in like 5 minutes. Please write back though if you would like to pursue more :-) hope so. Can't wait.

Hello. I am strongly drawn to you. I am also very aroused by the domination/hypnosis combination you offer.

I'm a novice and need training but do you use hypnosis?

With a good induction, I get turned on just by hearing words like: *relax*, *sleep*, *deeper*, *blank mind* and *mindless* being drilled into my open mind. Teased to follow and follow to be teased is also very sexy. For example, "Come with me. Follow me deeper into your mind. It feels so good when you follow me down. Follow me down, down, and down, deeper and deeper. The more you let go, the wetter I get. The wetter I get the deeper down you go. Let me deep into your mind. It feels so good to be in your head. Touching you deeply. Feeling you let go to my control. Let my thoughts become your thoughts. Your thoughts are my thoughts. Focus on my words as you drift away. My words are your thoughts. My words feel so good to you. You want my thoughts to fill your sleepy head. You obey my words. You must obey my words because they are your words. My words command you to sleep, deeper and deeper. Oh yes, my words feel so good. I'm filling your mind with my sexy little thoughts. Oh what I want to do with you my good little slave boy." Again, this is just an abbreviated induction in my own words. It would need Goddess' touch. I would happily call if you consider conditioning me (taking control). Or I could

*make a purchase of your choice, to prove my sincerity. Your one video ends "obey & submit to Mistress"... oh PLEASE, YES, **please** let me, Mistress. If you are interested, here is some info. I find you both very beautiful and very sexy, especially your face & cleavage. I like building intensity, some tease & denial. It sounds like some of your photos/video/cam may be partly nude... if so I would not want to see that at first (for tease & building intensity/desire). I have a submissive streak and hope you to use that (take control). Although you decide what I do & when, I would like to try email first, plus any teasing items you choose. If we still click, moving up to your recording or any teasing (but not revealing) photos or videos. Then maybe a live call with revealing photos. Then maybe a cam-call (still dressed but could tease me as much as you like). Anyways, that's the general idea. I await the pleasure of your reply*

Twisted Phone Sex

Hi beautiful. I was looking at your profile. Do you do hypnosis sessions on webcam? Because I would love to be hypnotized by your beautiful breasts and turned into your hypnotized slave. I have a breast fetish and a hypno fetish. I would love to set up an appointment if you're available. Email me back here or IM me at xxxxxx

Hello, I recently attended a party where a hypnotist was doing informal hypnosis demonstrations since that time I have become very interested in the thought of being hypnotized as I was watching the volunteers being hypnotized I was beginning to feel what the hypnotist was saying like heavy and such. After the party I went on the internet to find out all I could about being hypnotized that's what led me to this keen service I will tell you I've tried a couple of other listings but was not interested as it did not seem the same as that evening at the party. I've read your bio and understand the difference between hypnosis and

Twisted Phone Sex

Mistress Candice

erotic hypnosis I THINK I will tell you that the thought of being hypnotized does arouse me I hope that's normal. if you are available later this evening I would love to give it a try I do have a web cam so you can use it if you wish thank you for your consideration

I'd like to do a hypnosis-session with you on cam. Will you be on cam soon??

Your hypno-slave

70

I'm home alone for most of the day and was wondering if you wanted to make me your slave boy! lol It would be great to be hypnotized by you, forced to stroke for you, and pay you $100 whenever I cum. Maybe you could even be so evil as to hypnotize me into watching porn all day, and to call you whenever you send me an IM and pay you another $100 to cum! You can do this all night if you want lol! I'm all yours I don't check email that much, but if you want immediate servitude, send me an internet message.

Do you use NLP and Binaural technology? I find with my analytical mind that these techniques are very effective. Let me know if you are interested in more information. Until then, have a wonderful evening,

Twisted Phone Sex

I'd love to be taken into deep hypnosis live, but it will have to remain a fantasy for now. In the meantime, I am impatiently waiting to hear more hypnotic recordings. Your voice is so entrancing and your images only stimulate my curiosity further

Please let me know if you feel you can hypnotize me without being aware of it. I am very analytical and have a problem relaxing. If you can do it please let me know, I will call you

Twisted Phone Sex

I have had this fetish for quite some time and when I have seem men put under by a voluptuous vixen swinging a charm/pendant in front of her luscious cleavage have always desperately wanted to be the man in that predicament. particularly, if the man can be post-hypnotically triggered whenever he is "home-alone" for instance to obey the Mistress's (Your) commands, using webcam. I would also like to be triggered whenever I see a young (18-35 yr old) busty Woman wearing a tight-fitting horizontally striped black/white or red/white top to assume I am imprisoned inside Her; whenever I step out of the shower to imagine I see an image of me dressed in a corset, accentuating quite large cleavage and most importantly, in the winter months, be compelled to wear panties under my work clothes and sports bras underneath my shirt and jumper, without any conscious knowledge of doing so! I already have quite a collection to aid in this-one blue and one red sports bra; black one piece swimming costume as well as a stars and stripes one; a naughty maid outfit; red and black striped stocking, although buying a black and white one would be even better; yellow bikini, red fishnets and chocolate

Twisted Phone Sex Mistress Candice

colored ones, a wig (long hair), red peek-a-boo and 'covered' teddies. I use tennis balls for breasts, which I would like to think can be improved upon. Recently I tried to get rid of my useless dick by concreting it-a VERY painful experience. Have tried several times to sticky tape it up, but with time, its usefulness wanes. Sometimes calls can be very soft, I am single, never married as I have a great deal of difficulty in learning to trust people, although I'm sure you will be able to make me "see" differently with You! I am not really into the cocksucking side of things. I'm not sure which instant messenger you use but perhaps that could be a good way of sending me the post-hypnotic instructions. My user ID is XXXX if you are interested and it also tells you a couple of things-my first name and initial of my surname, plus where I am from-Australia, Sydney to be exact. Also, I would like to know with wearing golden hoop earrings, whether you need to have your ears pierced, as I have heard that can be quite painful. Hoping to slowly be transformed into your loving pet and you may like to give me a Woman's name that will be the trigger to take me into a very deep trance, from which you can further reprogram my mind into what you consider would be more suitable from a female viewpoint, to be switched on whenever I put on female clothes when at home alone. Then I can become one of your bevy of mindless slaves that you can control with even the click of your fingers. My E-mail address is <u>XXXXX</u>. Today I was upgraded to Super Fast broadband-vastly better than the 512k I have been battling with to date. I also have a very basic webcam, which will hopefully be able to accommodate motion better. I was wondering if it is "normal" to forget consciously your commands that are given to you while under hypnosis. I'm sorry this is tending to be long, but I'm hoping to get this out of the way so I don't have to waste valuable phone and cam time. Thanks and looking forward to doing all the exciting things you have planned for me.

Twisted Phone Sex

Mistress Candice

Can you do me a hypnotic voice recording as follows: You hypnotize me and I shrink down to 2 cm high. Then you play with my little penis very gently and tell me how you like to squish little guys, especially between your breasts, or sitting on them, or swallowing them, or feeding them to your pussy etc. etc. Then you show me, by doing it to other shrunken men. Lastly you pick me up and choose one of the above ways to finish me off. I like to hear descriptions of how you feel, and how the guys feel and I like to hear about their excitement, pain and futile struggling. This something you'd consider?

Twisted Phone Sex

I am hoping to find someone who is able to make my fantasy of wearing woman's clothing and diapers a reality through hypnosis. Is this possible or am I wasting my time. I also don't like being yelled at and like a soothing mothering tone of voice.

I hope I could find something about mind control. It must be fantastic to be brainwashed by your voice, so that there is no choice but to worship and tribute you on a regular base. But that's just, what I like. What do you like to create?

Twisted Phone Sex

Mistress Candice

I'd like to be gradually lured into a phone chat, and then deeply relaxed and encouraged under hypnosis to go on a sex-for-pay binge...is this something you can do?

Can you hypnotize me and plant a post hypnotic suggestion so that whenever I see a woman wearing stockings and high heels I will feel even more submissive to her? Also, if you included a suggestion that I would have to approach her and tell her how beautiful she is/ how sexy her legs are/ or how submissive I am to her/ or whatever you think would be appropriate and realistic... Feeling devious? Feel free to have some fun with this, too! I don't mind if you make a fool out of me, a little humiliation would do me good! Thanks, if it works, I'll be sure to report back to you my experience, and call for reinforcement!

P.S. I've had other hypnotists try this with various levels of success... It'll work for awhile and wear off. When the compulsions are strong, it's such an amazing feeling to give in and do exactly as I've been conditioned.

Twisted Phone Sex

Hi MISTRESS,

You have been extremely busy the last weeks ??? I like to be wrapped around your perfect finger and to fall completely under your spell! Just for you I want to go deeper and deeper.... With every snap of your finger ...I am looking forward to be spell bounded by your next mp3.

For years I've had a fantasy about being totally hypno-dominated by a beautiful, and feminine woman.

Twisted Phone Sex
Mistress Candice

For the life of me, I don't have a clue as to where it came from but it's a very persistent fetish. I've gone to my web browser over the years, and attempted to find someone who could make that dream a reality; but to no avail. It always seemed promising in the beginning, but the fantasy never did materialize; no matter how many MP3's I've tried. Frankly, it may be that I expect too much from these individuals and I've started thinking that maybe I should probably tone down my expectations. Then, while browsing I discovered you. After viewing your website, and reading the text: my hopes were soon rekindled. I'm sure that the fact that you are a stunningly beautiful woman; had nothing to do with it. :) My hope is maybe, just maybe; I have a chance of obtaining something that I had previously failed miserably at experiencing. I know that you probably deal with a multitude of strange personalities on a daily basis, and I don't want add to your burden. However, I would love the opportunity of speaking with you on the telephone but before I do; I would like to describe my fantasy to you. It may give you an indication as to whether you wish to speak with me, or not. If you discover that you don't wish any further contact; then I certainly understand. If you do, however, I would be a very ecstatic man.

Twisted Phone Sex

I had an idea where I asked you out on a date. I had no idea that you were a trained hypnotist. By the end of the date, you could tell that I really liked you, but you didn't think you'd want to date me a second time. On the date, you're wearing fashion jeans and a really trendy hooded zippered sweatshirt, but with nothing under it, and through the night, you've lowered the zipper a few inches, to see if I'd notice but, you were curious as to what I looked like, and what you might be giving up. So, while at your apt., you hypnotize me to do the following:

1. undress for you, while thinking I'm still dressed
2. Do jumping jacks and run in place for you
3. Make me measure everything down there for you, very accurately
4. Tell me to put rubber bands around my privates, so that you can see things better
5. You tell me that even though you'll date other guys, I'll not have the urge to date anyone else unless I ask your approval first.
6. You tell me, that from now on, I won't ever wear underwear, and I won't be able to explain why. And, anytime online, you say the word, "checking" I'll go on cam and prove that I'm doing it.

7. You tell me that I won't ever masturbate again, unless I get an approval from you. I have to ask nicely, and I have to be prepared to ask while naked on cam, and while on my knees.

8. You tell me that every time I try looking at your cleavage, I will feel a fairly nasty electric shock feeling in my testicles, and I feel the urge to tell you about it each time.

9. From now on, anytime you tell me to "measure" I have to measure my penis on cam, and give you a super accurate measurement, even if I'm small.

I won't remember doing any of these things, but the suggestions last forever. Do you do the trigger word thing so when u say that word I will become all yours?

My fantasy is this: I meet a beautiful woman who is dressed in stiletto high heels; wearing a full-length evening gown of satin, velvet or buttery soft leather. With that gown she would have matching opera length gloves; a full length mink coat; dripping with diamonds; heavily made-up, and wearing a most intoxicating perfume. Her speech, her gestures; her entire demeanor is thoroughly feminine, and deceptively innocent.

Her form of hypno-domination is slow, soft, and iron clad. Her control is sensuous, seductive; almost maternal in its approach. In the end, though, I become completely and irreversibly enslaved by her. She then reinforces her control by conditioning me to become aroused at the mere sight of her, and/or the sound of her voice. She conditions me to experience very real intense erotic daydreams, and to experience the same when asleep. She strengthens her control by instilling various fetishes; by which she uses them to manipulate me and control my behavior. When home alone, I would have the never-ending compulsion to become aroused by, and to be compelled to masturbate to your image. I wish to be completely; thoroughly and irreversibly possessed by you via hypnosis. This is my ultimate fantasy, and it is my hope that you don't find it to be offensive. My wish is that you will accept me for hypno-domination training. Thank you.

Twisted Phone Sex

Mistress Candice

Back in college I knew a woman, who was blisteringly hot and sexy and she wanted me. But there were two things that held me back - one was that she was with another guy, a very rich guy, and she made it plain that I wouldn't be anything more than sex to her and it would be at her whim. The other thing is that she was pretty much a bitch, getting away with everything because she was so hot. Of course, as time has gone by, she is pretty much all I think about these days. Can you put me under, and convince me that she is in front of me, taking me for her pleasure despite my hesitation/protestation? Can you make it so I see and feel her fucking me for her pleasure...

Twisted Phone Sex

You are a very sexy woman and I really enjoyed being your hypno-whore:) I would love to do a call with you however I am in Australia, which is GMT + 10, and this makes it difficult for us. I am available Monday Tuesday nights my time, which I fear may be a bit difficult for you, and also will be available on the weekend of 16 or 17 June, midday my time. Let me know if any of these times suit. My interests are femme dom, forced bi, feminization training, all under hypnosis. Thanks for the photos and something for me to strive for lol

Do you force femme, even when begged not to? Kevin still wants to be macho, but I like being girlie, sounds confusing, but I have been hypnotized many times.

Twisted Phone Sex

Hi

I'm interested in the erotic hypnosis but just wondered how long it generally takes to fall under the spell. That way I know how long my wife has to be out the house for hehe. Would 15 minutes be ok or is it more like 30 minutes?

How much time should I allow when you hypnotize me into your robot sex slave? Thank you

If I paid, could you do a hypnotic baby oil show?

If you use hypnosis there is no choice in being made a slave?

I would like to experience being a hot, young sexy woman ... can you do that

Hi goddess, sorry to bother ya but I am so in need of verbal abuse, being laughed at, spit on, called names, tease and denial, and all that cruel bitchy attitude, are you able to get me major addicted? again I have started to get weak and am falling for the addiction, the meaner and bitchier the weaker I get, I have been thinking about your power for the past 2 weeks, imp so glad you hypnotized me, kneeling, please take my life over goddess, kneeling,

abuse me. After four months of off an on, I broke from her fearing a slippery slope that I could still control. A 55 yr old nurse found me and was very sadistic. She force fisted me and disabled me from having normal sex again. She wants to eventually castrate me and double fist me so I have to wear diapers. I still have one foot in the "normal" world but no one will date me...all my friends have deserted me and I scroll for 24/7 slave positions. I was put in chastity once by the

Twisted Phone Sex

Mistress Candice

nurse but it slipped off in the shower. She always said that I would be hers and tomorrow, after a year, I'm offering my pathetic penis for encasement. I resist less and less and I truly feel that I will become those worthless, destroyed, pathetic males that no one really wants. I also desire to be a toilet for her and admitting that to a gorgeous woman like you is so humiliating. I will run from her when I sober up and I wish to be coerced into going through with slavery to this nurse Mistress. Will you help, please? Your seductive beauty and your hypnosis skills could crush me and emasculate me forever. I'm for real

Twisted Phone Sex

Mistress,

I downloaded your brainwashing MP3 and some other samples and I fear I might be stuck for the first time. I've tried other hypno Dom sites but either it caught up to me or something is in your recording that has me stuck on you. I live in LA...do you do real time play and which city are you in? I am searching for ongoing training/ruin from one Dom only. I'm single, live alone and wish to live in chastity while being enslaved mentally. You are gorgeous and I could slip into your oblivion. I've never been hypnotized and I'm a bit scared...what do I do now?

Twisted Phone Sex

Mistress Candice

I quite enjoy your profile and was wondering what type of hypnosis would be best for me, or for us to do on a call. I'm 29 and married to a woman who is 24 and lately have found myself wanting to watch her get fucked by another man. Usually it's my friend Chris, and she undresses him, sucks him for awhile, and then he has his way with her while I am told to watch and jerk off. My wife is shy in reality, so I could only experience this through hypnosis. Just wondering if you felt it would be worth exploring.

Thanks

I love all of the mp3s I have from you. But are you ever going to make one for married guys? Something along the lines of leaving the wife, job, family for you? Cheating on the wife by listening to you? Being devoted to you while maintaining the facade of a husband? I think that would be really hot. Thank you for the many hours of pleasure you have already given me.

Twisted Phone Sex

Mistress Candice

Hi. Been a while since we spoke, but would love to chat to you again and hopefully be hypnotized by you. I've always had a fascination with hypnosis and the idea of being hypnotically seduced by a sexy lady. Now for me it's always been more seductive and subtle where you hypnotize me, without me necessarily releasing it or even instantly, so that you can use me for whatever purpose you like (which is basically to seduce me!) I've also always had a fascination with jewelry and its role in hypnosis. I find watches and rings very sexy and arousing. Perhaps you use them to hypnotize me or as a trigger once I'm hypnotized so that I do things to you when I see your watch flash before my eyes, or your pendant wrapped around my cock, without necessarily knowing why. It would be good to chat to you if any of this is of interest to you. Otherwise, sorry to disturb!

Hi beautiful. I was looking at your profile. Do you do hypnosis sessions on webcam? Because I would love to be hypnotized by your beautiful breasts and turned into your hypnotized slave. I have a breast fetish and a hypno-fetish. I would love to set up an appointment if you're available.

Twisted Phone Sex

Hi, I was hoping to catch you today for a hypnosis session since we both seem to be around today :) Other ideas that I love (in addition to the below):

- reinforcing being a chronic masturbator and the need to masturbate lots
- only allowed to cum in humiliating ways (sniffing panties, humping a pillow, chanting a mantra, etc...)
- making me sexually dysfunctional/less desirable in other ways
- (and obviously) reinforcing my dick is small and cums so quickly.
- I adore cumming under hypnosis too :)

I have no real limits but I'm not really into financial domination. I am however, willing to pay more for custom recordings (on NF or MP3 sessions) if you are into either of those!

please, begging please get me addicted and brainwash me, I'm in love with ass and your voice, I want to be trapped in a world of addiction , I also love the controlling attitude, will call in a min, love pics,

Please let me know if you feel you can hypnotize me without being aware of it. I am very analytical and have a problem relaxing. If you can do it please let me know, I will call you.

Is it possible to combine domination with hypnotic? I like humiliation, tease/denial and financial domination. Is this possible to combine with hypnotic?

Your slave,

My fantasy is to surrender to your sorceress magic as you zap me with fire flying from your fingertips.

Twisted Phone Sex

I have an idea for a good trance session . You should do a bi session were the woman and men share the same cock but in the beginning the man is straight and the woman changes all that . Not a cuckold session just a bi session were the woman takes her boyfriend into sucking cock and loving it and sharing it with her.

Wow You are incredibly professional I am incredibly impressed I am fairly new to this site and You look like the real deal. Do You do text trance or PPV hypno games?

Twisted Phone Sex

Mistress Candice

I've never had a phone session & am saving my dollars for one with you. Since I feel I'm a difficult subject I wouldn't want to cut the session short because of the lack of money. I want to give you every opportunity to possess me completely, so this may take some time. I DO want You to hypnotize me & if I could experience what it would be like to automatically carry out one of Your post hypnotic suggestions without realizing I was doing it, it would convince me that I was Your's completely.

Sorry to bother you Mistress Candy but wanted to ask as your listing has had my interest for some time. I am a bit nervous about the whole hypnosis thing but it also sounds very wonderful. I was curious is there are any listings/records one should listen to first before making a call with you? Or if you had any advice. I must say you are extremely beautiful and have though about calling you a lot recently. Thank you kindly for any advice

help Goddess, I almost called a TS to talk to them. some of them look fantastic but I just couldn't do it with out asking You first if it was alright

Ok I am a bit nervous about this but find myself attracted to hypnosis. Divorced recently and looking to explore my submissive side. Maybe some anal play, not exactly sure. Hoping to be put under hypnosis and to explore the depths of my own mind influenced by your thoughts and words. To give up total control as my becomes your remote control toy in a way. Helping me explore through your words, wishes and commands. I can relax and usually put myself into a meditative thought so figure I can be put under quite easily.

Twisted Phone Sex Mistress Candice

can you hypnotize me into masturbating for you and while I masturbate I loose all my will and when I orgasm I am your mindless sex slave. please reply now and I will call now. You have me waiting in the hotel room, already dressed and blindfolded as you transform the other sissy whore in the bathroom.

You bring her out and place her on her knees with her eyes shut, then you guide me to my knees and put us face to face on our knees you tell us we must kiss and use our tongues and as we are doing that, you remove my blindfold. What do I see? What does she see? How do we look? Then you drive us somewhere, putting us in the backseat and telling us we must make out heavily and have oral sex until we get where you are taking us. Finally we arrive at the tattoo parlor and you guide us inside, forcing us to hold hands while you lead the way. You have us get humiliating and degrading tattoos and then thank the artist the way two sluts like us with no money would have to. what happens next? Can you take me through this fantasy?

Hi goddess, I was very interested in listening to you brainwash me into ass addiction, talking about how bad I want to worship ass, work for ass, be verbally abused, hypnotized by your voice as u talk about how obsessed I will be over your ass and not be able to look at any asses, I have a major ass fetish, can u brainwash me into sever ass addiction, I love g-string, smooth asses, being laughed at, controlled, verbally abused, being suckers and addicted, please advice,

ill pay before the session for text trance and obviously throughout the session with Your hypnotic powers You could probably make me pay more or PPV games with hypnosis involved. do You have more hypnotic pics? I am a sucker for hypno pics too My fetishes from biggest to smallest are.....Nails, hands, jewelry, hypnosis, brainwashing, mind manipulation, ass worship, foot worship, witchcraft, spellbinding, financial domination forced intoxication, kind of like blackmail, but more like full control of my life, like access to everything and basically being a little puppet/pawn

I am fairly new to this site and have only visited one girl and she wrote a story for me. I can't use the phone much because of my girlfriend.

thank You for Your time

wish You were here I need You. I've started looking at transgender and it scares me that I like it. I know You will tell me if it's ok. I trust You but it does seem a little odd

I was wondering if you could make me a short (non-hypnosis or hypnosis) companion file to play when I'm masturbating that drives home some of the points in the hypno file. I masturbate a lot lately, especially when XXXX denies me sex or blowjobs, sometimes in the next room when she's asleep and it would be amazing to have something that I could listen to on my ipod while I did. Anyways, if you don't want to, that's cool too, but if you can think of something that might work, I'll happily pay the extra for it.

Twisted Phone Sex Mistress Candice

I long to gaze into those devastating hypnotic green eyes and be swept away by that mesmerizing voice to where ever it is you send me. Hope for a trip to hypnotic paradise tomorrow.(Thursday) Don't know when you are reading this just want to make sure we are talking about the same time. I know you are not on now anyway my wife is home.

I already have the make up and everything applied, it would probably be best to just touch on this area , stating the fact that I enjoyed applying it etc, and spend most of the time in the area of what I have shown below.

Hi...I've emailed u a couple of times but haven't heard back from you. Are you around to play tomorrow (Monday)? I want to get a chastity trigger added.

Twisted Phone Sex

Mistress,

Thank you for reading my email. I have always had a fantasy of being put under hypnosis and being hypnotized to fall in love with a Mistress. The Mistress plants trigger words that when I hear them I get an instant erection, and another trigger that makes me cum uncontrollably. Is this something you could do. I would like to give up control to a Mistress with that power.

If I dressed as a girl completely with make up dress etc. Maybe go down a track of as I look at myself as a girl , I will feel more and more like a girl, an see myself more as girl. I will realize that I don't want to take my make up off.

Twisted Phone Sex

Mistress Candice

If I start thinking I need to take my make up and dress off now , I will think of reasons why I shouldn't, and realize that I don't won't to. This will make me feel very excited , the more excited I get the more I feel I don't want to take off my make up etc off, and this will me even more excited, and make want to take it off less and less. (If I think again I should take this make up off now, I will again think of reasons why I shouldn't , and possible make me want to put on more make up ,perfume, or try on other dresses.) I start to realize that I am trapped as a girl , and this excites me even more, but also makes me want to leave it on even more. If I climax it will lock in more feelings of pleasure , and make me even want to leave it on even more. I am not sure how to end it , maybe I wake up the next morning , and then I can take it off then.??? Let me know what you think

Can you put me under and make me cum every time I hear the phrase "Memorial Day?"

My Goddess and Mistress, I have drained and made room for you my Wicked Hypnotist, My will is yours I will do anything you ask, I am at your beacon call forever. I have never even thought of this before will you take my ass with your strap on and take my virginity, I beg of you my Goddess I will do anything for you

Twisted Phone Sex Mistress Candice

Hi Candice. Do you remember me? If you put me under what kind of naughty dangerous triggers could you give me? maybe one where if I masturbate and cum it drains ALL of my maleness out. Then you could dictate how I would be until my balls filled again in 2-3 days.. What triggers would work on me as a sissy with my balls empty...?

Hi Goddess,

I have been browsing Your site and listened to Your samples and I would love to have a live session with You, so would You be interested in thinks like hypnosis, brainwashing, mind control, making me addicted, dominating me, taking advantage of me and giving me suggestions for Your benefit? I'm 27 years old and from Finland so please forgive me my sometimes bad English..

possibly making things so difficult or uncomfortable when I don't have them on so that I'm pretty much forced to wear them to make myself feel normal. I have also had desires of using hypnosis to control me and make me confess to wearing pantyhose to people if certain words where spoken or anything that would want to make me feel like I had to blurt it out. I hope you understand what I'm trying to explain to you and if so maybe you can tell me if this is really possible through hypnosis to truly make my life difficult and addicted to pantyhose.

My wife will be here any min to pick me up for lunch, so I can not call. I have been listening to some of your mp3s and looking at your new photos and my cock is rock hard. Do you have any instructions for me before she gets here can I stoke my cock? Should I call you later and tell you what happened at lunch?

Twisted Phone Sex Mistress Candice

wanting to become completely yours, I do not want you to let me cum. I want you to take me so deep and do anything you want with me install all the triggers you want and need and make me do things I would never even thank of doing. Goddess please take me and do things to me and make me do things I would never dream of but do not let me cummmmm, make me suffer. Please let me know if you become available today

I need to work on my visualization as we discussed. What I see is either abstract or like a still photo that is there and gone in a flash. Sometimes I see in black and white and sometimes in color. Instead of seeing myself walk down the spiral stairs, I see my mind's eye follow the shape of the smooth spiral slide all the way down. I feel warmth, tingling, heaviness, and immobility. I even feel myself filling with your light and radiating it when commanded. I never feel like I'm moving except maybe sinking into the velvet cushion when commanded.

Erotic Power Exchange: I have a great need to please and GIVE up control voluntarily but think I'm still a little scared that hypnosis could take my control and not give it back. I know it's silly but that's how I feel. I like humiliation in the form of being forced to do humiliating things like forced fem, shopping assignments, or whatever turns you on. I don't want to be insulted or degraded. On the contrary, I want to be praised for my humiliating behavior if I've pleased you and have you point out how you can tell I like my humiliation and shouldn't I be ashamed at enjoying it? I think this is a mind game you can have some fun with I hope.

Chastity: I don't want to be locked in a cage (scary, uncomfortable, no erections) but I'm open to other forms of cock control. I know you've already started me down this path and I'm loving it so far even though it's distracting me from getting things done around the house. lol I've been a big fan of T&D for awhile now. Of course hypnosis would seem to make a cage unnecessary. If you wanted you could get the same effect with only a single pink ribbon tied loosely in a pretty bow around the base of my package or nothing at all. But I still prefer being hard and horny all the time and only able to cum for you with your permission. I'm even starting to look forward to the day when you can give me a single command to make my cock, hard, soft, cum, cartwheels, a little dance, or whatever else you want. lol Even before I discovered erotic hypnosis I had a fantasy of a cock cage that would only make my erections bigger, harder, and more sensitive but unable to cum. I even wondered what wearing something like that would do to my dreams if I wore it while sleeping. I think that's why I bought a cage. I wanted to know what would happen to my dreams if something stopped me from getting erections in my sleep (I hear it's normal to get erections during sleep every night).

Gender bending: Even though I am not naturally a cross dresser or want to be a woman, my past experience has taught me that I love to be force feminized. By submitting to this it pushes a lot of my buttons, giving up power and control, submitting, obeying, surrendering, pleasing my mistress, humiliation, and the feel of silk isn't bad either. lol I think you said this is one of your favorite fetishes. If so, then I'm ready to become whatever you want to make me. With erotic hypnosis we can really go wild with this one. You can be my naughty nurse or evil doctor and transform me with hypnotic drugs, kinky equipment, or any other wild ideas you can dream up. I still don't want a real life sex change but in hypno fantasy land you could give me triggers to make me think I was a hot slutty female cocksucker, a bisexual she male sex slave, myself trapped in a woman, or even isolate the female part of my mind so that I could meet the girl inside to see what she's like. What kind of girls do you like to play with? Cheerleaders? Dumb as a dildo bimbo? Strong corporate woman in suits and translucent white blouses that almost hide their sexy lingerie? I can't wait to see what you want to do with me.

Sucking Cock: I think this is another thing that you like in a slave if I remember right. I think I might be ready to learn how to suck cock for you and here's why. A few years ago when I was in

Twisted Phone Sex   Mistress Candice

XXXXXX's web slave training class, she was disappointed that I was straight and didn't like guys or sucking cock. I really hated disappointing her (there's that need to please again) so it started me thinking... I assume all straight men fantasize that all women are bisexual. It only stands to reason that all straight women would want all men to be bi also. If true, I would be a disappointment to any domme in this area. I think that's when I decided that I could become a better slave if I could learn to be more flexible in this area. Some time later when I discovered erotic hypnosis I stumbled across Mind Mistress's web site which has a lot of free hypno stuff designed to make anyone who views it into a happy cocksucker. I did all the free stuff and found that it did have a positive impact on me. For example, seeing men kiss, have sex, whatever, doesn't make me cringe and make my skin crawl any more. Now I'm just neutral. It doesn't bother me at all but it doesn't turn me on either. The other thing it did was give me a whole new interest at watching beautiful girls sucking on big, hard, juicy cocks. I especially like to see bright red lips wrapped around the tip so I can still see part of the head and the whole shaft. Sexy makeup, good eye contact, and of course nice boobs is great too. It's funny how a hard cock can suddenly become fascinating if it's got the right mouth attached to it. lol I don't expect to suck any real cocks in real life and glory holes just seem stupid and dangerous to me, but I can see me becoming your good little cocksucker in our private little hypno fantasy world some day. I don't know what tricks you have up your sleeve to help corrupt my mind in this direction but I have a few ideas you might find helpful, but I suspect you already know all this stuff better than I do. I love the idea of you fucking me in the ass with your strap on. I also have a fantasy of taking on 2 girls with strap on, DP type. Maybe you can get me started with toys and go from there. The second idea involves getting me hypnotically addicted to the taste of my own cum and going from there. The last idea is to set a trigger that temporarily turns me into a straight horny female slut. Girls love to suck cock so if I'm a girl, wouldn't that mean I love to suck cock too? I guess we'll find out. lol

Twisted Phone Sex

Mistress Candice

Medical fetish: Naughty Nurse, Evil Doctor, sounds, catheters, enemas, restraints, electrical play, forced orgasms, cyber implants, hypno drugs, etc. There's not much in this category I don't want to try short of castration. I love my package far to much to loose it even in hypno fantasy. This is another area where hypno fantasies can really run wild.

I'd love to hear about any or your fantasies that you want to try with me, especially anything new and different that you've never done before or haven't found anyone willing to try it with you.

Man, still really long winded but hopefully more coherent than my last mess.

How about this? You hypnotize me to watch porn and stroke, but not be able to cum until I first call you and submit to your stroking instructions and a tease and denial call of whatever length you want. Plus in order to cum, I have to pay you an additional $100. After it's all done, you wipe my memory clean, and make me do it all over again, as many times as you want. Let me know if it sounds fun. IM me on yahoo or eyeball, I'm munson13 there, and I'll come running!

Hello, as you can see by my user name I am little dicked sissy. My sissy name is Julie and my given name is Julius. I have never been hypnotized, but have this feeling that I would like to be. I would like to feel like a woman when I touch myself and I thought maybe I could achieve that through hypnosis. I have always masturbated a lot and have never had any penis power, always cumming too quickly and never pleasing any ladies with my teeny weenie. I was a bed wetter well into my teen years and even now sometimes I can not control my bladder and pee myself. My last girl friend called me a prissy sissy and my ex wife gave me my nick name her little dicked sissy boy. That is a little about me, do you think you can hypnotize me? Please tell me what you think and if I should call you or not. Thank you,

Your hypnosis is so wonderful! I have enclosed some of my sissy pictures for you to enjoy. I look forward to actually talking to you in person. Many sissy kisses in my pretty panties, Remember Don't let me cum Goddess, but place all the hypnotic triggers you want in me

As long as you promise to make me your hypno toy and slut and make me do things I never imagined doing under your spell. Make me due anything you want and desire my Goddess, I am a hypno virgin and very vulnerable. Been listening to your 4 sessions that I have bought and the 2 you gave me almost everyday. cant wait for more and more. always at your beckon call.

I was thinking of an induction idea where You suck on a lollypop and as we listen, we feel our minds being sucked away. It becomes harder to think as we become more aroused, while You suck away more of our thoughts.

Submissively,

Hello ... I am a Sissy with a little extra I have lost some weight and also I have add some implants and I am in search of some one who can have me be more fem and more of a care free slut.. Although a real women would never really be called slut I hope you would know what I mean... I will wait for a reply before calling you... I am into **Hypnosis**

Twisted Phone Sex

Mistress Candice

Its probably an hour since my call and I'm losing my mind. Have been listening to mindless hunter and breast obsession mp3s and normally after I call you, you have me aching to have sex with every woman I see.

Twisted Phone Sex

After one of our sessions you took my "hair fetish" to all time heights. I almost totally lost it at this meeting with another attorney here who was playing with her hair while exposing her cleavage. But now, after talking today, I'm concurrently sort of excited by the usual things but mostly I'm completely demoralized and just want to hear you and not bother with them. Ug its so hard. Please please please help. Don't know what happened today. Have the most intense mental images of you from today's call. But the most fun parts of what you do to me was always you forcing me to have this constant spiral of lust to bed every woman I see and then every woman making me want you more. Now I just feel aching for you, and am somewhat demoralized and conflicted about these other women I've been agonizing over. Please say you can help me? I'm a disaster over here. Am apparently at the point where I obviously just do whatever you tell me. Pretty sure you have complete and total control over me. But right now I feel so conflicted and messed up. please help? Or tell me what to do? Sigh.

Tonight I have tickets to a hockey game and asked my ex-girlfriend to go. She's hot looking and physically we've always been good. What I'm thinking is after being put under we add some consequences if my team (the NJ Devils) lose tonight. I'll give you some general guidelines so you get the gist but encourage you to add to it anything that increases the humiliation <blushing> factor...LOL If they lose (or even tie)....on the way home in my car I say how disappointed that they played like 'sissies'...and offer to strip and wear just HER panties home as punishment. I know her...she'll probably laugh and go along with that (if she's wearing any). Then several things can happen that would add to my embarrassment....including unwanted boners, and things I say like 'these feel better then I thought they would', or please don't tell anybody

this made me hard - I'll do ANYTHING', or 'I hope you don't think I'm a little sissy cause of this boner?' or 'thank god you're not taking pictures of this' or 'put some lipstick on me and I'd look like a girl' or 'I'm glad you weren't wearing a garter belt and stockings too or I'd probably be wearing them as well. After that I leave it to your erotically evil mind to add to my humiliation as long as I'm not arrested...my ex-gf is a little dominant so there should be no problem there (that could a problem in of itself LOL). The big risk that if the NJ Devils lose I'll be triggered to completely humiliate myself will make the game SUPER exciting...and drive home very memorable! I could request her to wear sexy undies tonight...that would be consistent with our relationship etc in case u have any ideas here...If they win...well maybe I'm off the hook (maybe not - I sorta like not knowing what triggers I have).

Twisted Phone Sex

Mistress Candice

hello Ma'am my name is XXX and I don't know if I can be hypnotized. I have listened to a few hypnosis recordings before and they have never done anything for me. is there something wrong with me?

Chapter Four

Responding to

Hypnosis

Some of the credit given to me by satisfied customers is earned and some is imagined. At times I do nothing more than parrot back to them the words they specifically asked to hear; other times I weave a complex custom fantasy in which they become the erotic star. Either way this feedback from their original calls emphasizes the pleasure they derived from this form of entertainment and reinforces and expands on the creativeness of the next call.

Twisted Phone Sex

Mistress Candice

Oh my god, just like last time, I am awestruck by your power, I haven't wanted sex so bad, ever, in my life. Every woman I see. Want so bad. And want you so much more. So intense, it's amazing. You're amazing .need to hear you so soon. I am dying to talk to you again. Everything you did to me worked so well, it's terrifying. But I can't quite seem to get away, or to get the time to call you in private. In my desperation, I've had a crazy idea. Do you think there's any chance I could pay you to create mp3 recordings for me? I've got a 30 minute train ride to and from NYC every day. It would be amazing if I could listen to recordings on the way to and from work. Hammer home all your suggestions. Obviously not force me to act while on the train, but would drive me insane nonetheless. The only time I seem to be able to get any quiet these days, is really early in the morning. It's awful! I am going nuts. I need to hear you so bad!!!

PS-- in the last two weeks, amazing things have happened. Talking to you is like a magic spell... was completely life altering. Now I'm just dying to hear you so bad, it aches... What do you think?

Twisted Phone Sex

I have been seeing you when my wife and I kiss and snuggle. I have been seeing you when I try to go to sleep. But all within tolerable limits. But now you have sent me these two photos, and suddenly the blackboard and the word DESIRE on the blackboard are overwhelming. I have to have access to you. I've got to hear your voice. I've been awake most of this Tuesday night since getting your email Tues evening. Please tell me when you are going to be online today, Wednesday. I have appointments today, Wednesday, but I am going to have to break some of them if that is the only way to be online with you.

Twisted Phone Sex

Mistress Candice

I can't seem to get away... am dying to talk to you again. It's been so long!!!! Everything you did to me worked so well, it's terrifying. But I can't quite seem to get away, or to get the time to call you in private. In my desperation, I've had a crazy idea. Do you think there's any chance I could pay you to create mp3 recordings for me? I've got a 30 minute train ride to and from NYC every day. It would be amazing if I could listen to recordings on the way to and from work. Hammer home all your suggestions. Obviously not force me to act, while on the train, but would drive me insane nonetheless. The only time I seem to be able to get any quiet these days, is really early in the morning. It's awful! I am going nuts. Need to hear you so bad!!! Do you have any ideas? There was that blissful week or two where I was calling you several times a week. That was amazing. Now I just can't get away. I miss the intense and insane experience of calling you so much!!!!

126

My all-controlling SUCCUBUS,

I need to fuck you - not jerk off to you. I need to lose myself during a freckle-count with you on top, bucking madly away, seducing my life essence, smothering your tits in oil, brainwashing me with your soft whisperings of control. I need you so badly!

I bought some of your videos awhile back and my stupid roommate erased them. I was wondering if I could buy them again plus more!!!

In my continuing battle to fight your temptations, to avoid succumbing to your "phone slavement", (which would obviously result in the gradual

Twisted Phone Sex Mistress Candice

draining of my bank account), I am once again besieged by your machinations, Mistress, as I ecstatically beat myself off silly at the sight that YOU KNOW, you turn me on: in your newest photo - that nice, pearly stone, on that lovely diamond-studded choker, along with way you hold on to those big, fucking cock-devouring hooters of yours,............so fucking beautiful............even the way you hook those long-talented thumbs under your bra-straps like that, INSTANTLY "sprung" (like my cock - for you) to mind the hooks that you've so wickedly plunged through both this fucking beefcake's fucking testicles. One of my favorite "Beat Off For Goddess " fantasies - quite often when I'm hitting the sack - is when you work your wiles on guys on the internet, persuading them, especially the shy ones, (and ESPECIALLY the rich or v.i.p.s), to show you their dedication, to show you how you've managed to put those nasty 'old fish-hooks through each and every one of their nuts like you have with me, and entice them into camming their appreciation for you. With your instructions, they make up an "(idiot's name): Slave for Mistress" sign; make sure that their face is clearly in the cam's screen, and eventual ejaculation - as dramatic and manly as possible. Oh - and as they're about to come, you "program" them to say, repeatedly, "Obey Mistress......so I can come". Once you've told them that you've "documented" their cam performance for "future, if needed, use", you build and build your "Mistress Consortium", yes-men who are at your pussy whipping mercy, blue balled warriors only to happy to maintain your comfortable lifestyle.

More to so dearly cum and cum and cum,

Twisted Phone Sex Mistress Candice

Oh god, please help? Since our last session, I am losing my mind. I can't get away from the office to call you, and I keep touching myself constantly. Every time I see a remotely attractive woman at the office, I respond physically immediately, and then find a way to take care of that at work. Please please please help. There are one or two women at the office that I'm dying to actually... interact... with. Can we PLEASE make me do that instead of doing this? I'm in agony. Please help. I can't check keen from the office, but please email me if you have any suggestions. I'm dying. Almost terrified to call again!

Twisted Phone Sex

Guess what? I spent 2 hours in a peep show booth with a glory hole in an adult book store outside of Ann Arbor Michigan! I had my pants around my knees, put my ass up to the hole, stuck my tongue through it, and even ran my finger around it when it was occupied, but never got any cock, big sigh! But he could see me jacking off, and hear me moaning! I can't wait to go back!

Your filthy whore,

You are so strong, it's such an amazing feeling to give in and do exactly as I've been conditioned. Thank you very much Goddess... I've been waiting a long time to hear a full erotic induction from you. I hope to hear more.

Twisted Phone Sex Mistress Candice

I've had the opportunity to listen to this induction and feel a new-found devotion to you. You are very talented and I was deeply aroused and submissive during the entire session. It seems obvious that you have some professional training in hypnosis. If you have more untested works in the rough, I'd more than happy to give you feedback. ;) As for interests, it turns me on to go blank and lose my mind to a seductive hypno-mistress. Having your silky words sink deeply into my mind is so lustfully erotic to me. I also love triggers phrases that enforce deep trance and sexual arousal, and do so love orgasm control. Have a wonderful evening.

Submissively,

Goddess, that was awesome. My head is still swimming and swooning from the sound of your voice. It is very sexy and seductive. Like a siren's song. Just responding to you now is giving me such a tingle. ;) As for triggers, I enjoy feeling my conscious focus intensify on the hypnotist's voice to the point where I'm following each and every syllable intently. i.e. "The more you focus on my voice, the more mindless you become. The more mindless you become, the more you focus on my voice." To disable the critical faculties, the more I focus and become mindless, the more suggestible I become. Finger snaps and other jolting sound effects, shock me into a deeper state when used at surprising moments and followed by control commands. Sometimes a hypnotist uses phrases with a double meaning to invoke arousal and deepen trance at the same time. For instance, "The *harder* you try to think, the more mindless you become. The more mindless you become, the *harder* it is to think."

Twisted Phone Sex Mistress Candice

OMG it happened again several times today. I can't control myself. At my age I probably won't ever get to shoot all over anybody's tits but I go into a kind of frenzy when I see cleavage. I know that didn't happen before. Did you do something to me that I don't know about?

Hopelessly stiff, doing what I can to avoid phoning when you whenever you "fire up" the old' sperm factory of mine

OMG... I... wow... that's not, I mean... you're making it almost impossible to... I mean, it's... I feel like I'm on my last strand of will power to keep myself from calling you. I'm worried that when I actually do break down and call, you'll make me your bitch... and... I'm even more afraid that I'll want that to happen, and love it when you do make me your bitch...

Oh God Goddess this is awesome... way too much for my poor brains to resist... I know I must here everything because I always wake up with a mess but I don't think I can remember even half of what you said to me... I only know that whenever I see or hear you I'm immediately aroused to the brink of no return. Oh Goddess... please please has a little mercy on the simple brains of a poor submissive soul...

What are you trying to do, ruin me?

Hmmm, love your voice. I can't wait to call again.

Remarkable trance - as I apparently dropped my phone during the call

Oh God oh God this is too much... Damn you're good All I can think of is you and

Twisted Phone Sex Mistress Candice

You only, I can't seem to get You of my mind anymore. Somehow I have the feeling you tricked me somewhere and I probably should run like hell but ooohh God Goddess... You sound so sweet and seductive in my ears. I don't even can think strait anymore. You are so beautiful, so enticing, enchanting, your voice so pleasant and addictive... God do I love You... I'm afraid I'm losing my mind completely to Your seductions I can't resist this anymore, it's just to much to handle, I can't even run from this, Your picture's are in my mind all day, Your voice is in my head all day. Goddess.... oh Goddess... I just want to fall on my knees in submission and completely surrender to you. Please please Goddess take control of my life and let me be Your slave, I want to serve and obey You .totally... in anything I feel like nothing matters anymore only serving You Goddess... Please Goddess take complete

control of my life, I need You so much.. Oh Goddess I need and love you…There's only a small drawback, in a few hours I'm leaving for a 14 day vacation, probably I should have asked Your permission for this but I didn't know You when this deal was made and I can hardly bail out on the last minute.. only hope this feeling for you doesn't wear of in this time. Heavy sigh.....
I still don't know how you did it... Jeeeezzz Goddess you are unbelievable… a true divine enthralling Goddess
Sincerely Yours

Goddess I am so messed up now I can't make head or tails of my desire for you. I am nervous about buying this program I feel if I do I will be totally lost to my desire to serve you forever. Please make me go one way or the other the decision is Yours Goddess

Twisted Phone Sex Mistress Candice

I did like the "bitchtrain" mp3 you sent, and I love your voice! And, it scares the bejeesus out of me to even think of saying something that would make it seem like I'm not in complete appreciation and awe of you and your voice... I guess, I mean in the world I grew up in a "bitch" is... well, it's not really a "slave" in terms, but more in terms of a "sub" or some sort. I don't want to make this too wordy, and it's getting confusing and slightly dizzy even writing to you... but, I mean... you're so beautiful, so sexy, gorgeous, your voice is so sweet, smooth, seductive, alluring... you're irresistible. I could see myself being exploited, used, and even owned because it's easy to see how simple it would be to become completely addicted to you. And you using my addiction to have whatever type of control you wanted... and use me like a "bitch". Again, sorry for getting too wordy. Although, after listening to that mp3, I'm seriously in a fight to not go out and buy a pair of panties to wear for you...Well... I mean, it's just really tough to have enough will power to NOT do something that comes from your voice... form that perfect, gorgeous, soothing, irresistible voice... I'm just, I mean... I'm not a sissy really, or have any tendencies of that type of thing... maybe "bitch" is the wrong word... I'm not sure, it's just the first time I heard you say the word "bitch" it just seemed "right". Like, from your voice, it felt like a label that suited me for you.

I still feel like I'm in a trance. My body feels so heavy. I'm sort of scared, though. I was in a restaurant a few weeks ago and somebody said something and I made excuses and went home right away and listened to your recording. I've got such a crush on you. Is this an email of devotion? I'm not sure, not very good at these sorts of things. All I know is that you get inside my head and when you let me cum I cum so hard that I'm shaking afterward. It's hard to have sex with any other girls without thinking of you.

Twisted Phone Sex Mistress Candice

Thank you Mistress for the awesome mp3 tease and denial, it hurt so good. I felt so tingly all over in such a good trance/under your power then once I got to the teasing and stroking about half way through I finally came all over my chest. I didn't have enough will power or wasn't under enough to maintain control I guess. So I listened to the whole thing. It still had a very good deepening effect on my slave body I feel. So I will continue to train and listen to tantric worship and then tease and denial mp3's then I should be the perfect slave for you to mold into your liking Mistress. I will have to wait till probably Tuesday maybe sooner before I can call you again. As I will be busy. I am also getting ready to move to Denver. Then I will be driving a Semi truck over the road mostly western USA hopefully. I wish I met you somewhere other then here your body is the most amazing thing my eyes have seen. And your voice brings me to my knees where I belong; such a sexy voice you have Mistress. Thank you Mistress for everything you have done

Do you do anything to me I should know about? My cock keeps getting harder and swelling. It feels like all my blood in my body is rushing into my cock. It hurts badly. :(

Twisted Phone Sex   Mistress Candice

Okay okay okay I admit I tried to resist you but having a little bit of problems with that, BIG problems actually. With Your help I'm able to cum like never before, fireworks all around, without your help I can only get aroused everything else is a big no. Yes I have a big submissive streak, I love to be dominated by You Goddess, You are so unbelievable beautiful, Your voice so pleasant captivating erotic seductive and hot, angels in my ears, but this kind of control is something I just didn't expect behind Your pretty face. I kind of underestimated your abilities in this and now I have this problem that I just NEED you so bad Goddess if I want to cum at all... Heavy sigh.... Problems problems problems.... Life was so easy before...

Just your voice makes me long to obey. Looking at your pictures while listening I cannot deny you anything. Your voice is compelling; the combination of the voice and photos is overwhelming. I will always submit to Mistress.

Soft and sultry and oh so relaxing I love you Mistress.

Thank you Mistress for your mesmerizing pictures and voice I cherish you. I know I have no choice but to submit now. But that's ok I love it.

Thank you so much Mistress for the control I so badly need. I will always be in worship position for you Mistress.

Mistress you are amazing!!!! I was not myself all day after this call. You are so beautiful and dangerously clever. One moment I think: I'm in control and ok and the next moment I realize you have said something, somehow to really mess my brain up. I want to meet you in real life, but it could be way more than I can handle – You have warned me. Still I really want to do so someday. You are so sexy it is scary!!!

Twisted Phone Sex Mistress Candice

I am unable to resist anything you tell, make or ask me to do. I am so deeply controlled and in love I never want, or can resist anything you tell me to do.

This was relaxing and I love your voice, but it did not seem to hypnotize me and I did not cum. It may have not been ideal conditions as I was sitting in my chair stretched out and relaxed as best I could, but I did follow all instructions except that. I will try it again this evening while laying on my bed in the nude and see what happens.

Thanks very much for this test

Chapter Five

Appreciation and

Devotion

Sharing secrets without fear of judgment or criticism can make people feel more than simply comfortable with whom they share. Complete acceptance combined with protection of anonymity can instantaneously transform simple appreciation into devotion or even worship. For some the worship itself is the fantasy. The difference is subtle, but distinct, as you see. However, this can be a fickle lot. If they perceive the slightest of slights, whether real or imagined, they will abandon you quicker than any other type of client.

Twisted Phone Sex

Mistress Candice

Dear Mistress,

I couldn't be more pleased that you accepted my offer. I also feel just thrilled. And even more, thank You, generous Mistress, for choosing exactly the type of pictures I was hoping for. Your responses leave me eager and hungry for more. I feel a bit like going up the BIG hill on a rollercoaster. The anticipation is building. But more, awareness sinks in that it will be a long, thrilling descent deep into your seductive spell.

In anticipation,

I am SO intrigued by your various charms that I will adjust for you if necessary. Still, I'd rather delay a live call for a bit. You could charge more if needed, for your time & effort. I'd prefer a slower teasing/seduction via mail, photos, or other.

I hope to build a powerful sense of urgency, an almost desperate longing to talk to you. I confess I already feel quite a pull. I have a submissive streak but also like the usual male things, and hope you can mix all your charms to keep me coming back for some time. I see in you not just extraordinary physical beauty, but creativity, flexibility and a delightful sense of playful fun. If what I suggest just won't work for you, let me know and I will adjust as best I can.

Yours to command,

Dear Mistress,

WOW. Yes. YES. YES!! Oh how I like your email. Love it. My desire for you is strong and grows stronger. I am THRILLED you are sending more pictures. I want your pictures, all of them. I ache to see you in your sexy, teasing outfits. I ache to see your eyes looking right at me. Your exquisite, soul piercing eyes, beguiling, bewitching, enchanting me, riveting me in stunned, breathtaking adoration. Inviting me to fall, to dive within, not knowing or caring if I ever return. Sometimes with that knowing smile... knowing how I am sinking for you. Knowing with just this little taste, my initial intrigue is already growing to a hunger... and with each sampling, will grow beyond hunger. Thank you so much for the lovely, beautifully written email that rivets your name in my mind that drives my thoughts like gas on a flame. The email like a self fulfilling prophecy haunts me with your name and image, running wild & free in my mind. Please, Please let me continue showing my devotion

Your utterly spellbound servant,

Your words are delicious. I would be delighted if you continued milking me this way for a while. Though I am nervous about my ability to "hold back" my (Your?) release! I have some interests I want you to discover, even if you only act on those you like. Please, will you "extract" this from me?

Any method from tease/tempt/seduce, to forced confession, to sort-of-blackmail (such as, no more pictures until…).

Perhaps you have another way. Naturally, you may feel I must send extra "$-ugar" for this. …of course… it takes sugar to make you sweet ;) Your last 3 photos are superb. I am so, so, SO grateful you send the fully clothed pictures that teasingly draw & seduce me helplessly to you and make me ache for more… for many more. Such a sexy, seductive delicious vicious cycle, I plead with you to continue… please continue…

Twisted Phone Sex

Dear Mistress,

You blow me away. I see email in my inbox and feel a thrill that it's from you. I pause just a moment to let the mystery and excitement builds. Then I open it, hungry, almost helpless to stop myself. Even the higher price does not slow me. Then I read your words. AGAIN, more than I expect. And it may not even matter if they are sexually oriented or not.

You wrote absolutely wonderfully. Creative, lovely, seductive and willing to broach new & unexpected territory, I find you to be creative, soulful and unique amongst all women. I just ache to please you.

Beyond Your incredible desirability as a beautiful woman, you have more than skin deep beauty. I may be getting a crush on you. (More below...)

Your pictures were again amazing, ALL three. The real life shot is charming and gorgeous. And you have such a fabulous smile! You don't need cleavage to be tremendously attractive and inviting. But I felt the huge urge to write a bit from the other planet, from the submissive world. The shot of you on the bed, wearing

Twisted Phone Sex

boots and black and teasing by almost revealing your spectacular breasts... Oh GODDESS! That's the seductive, enticing come hither look you could make me do anything with. And your words, OH GODDESS your words! With what manner of magic do you bewitch me? I do feel I am getting lost, lost in your charms and your spell. As if You are leading me into the night, away from the well-lit world of the familiar, deeper towards the dark, into mystery, where it becomes harder to see anything but YOU. So please, please, Mistress, let me, make me follow you deep, deeper, and then far deeper still into YOUR incredible world. And oh... did I mention how much I want you? ;)

Just plain smitten,

Twisted Phone Sex

Dear Mistress,

Our arrangement is wonderful, I strongly want to continue. I should give my limits... All legal, no health risks, no public humiliation. You requested my photo, is it for your eyes only? Forgive me, but that leaves budget...For a lasting arrangement, $50/day tribute plus phone calls (I won't want to rush)... is a problem. Can we please work something out? A pace I can sustain? Possibilities (Your ideas welcome)

1) $50/day until phone call release. Then start a new chapter. Start each chapter at a low price, but, you control increases, even several, as the chapter unfolds. You decide how & when chapters end.

2) Less pictures per email or, only in alternate emails?

3) Email tributes back to $25/30 or so

4) Might these or some other work for you? (I like 1 better than 2)

Your phone rate is fine.

Twisted Phone Sex Mistress Candice

When are you going to be available, I think your so beautiful and the sexiest women on earth

Dear Completely Captivating Goddess,
I am 1 day behind in tribute. Please may I catch up, oh haunting Mistress of Desire? I should have known – you are so good you can be habit-forming. And I am getting so addicted.
Your charmed, chaste, craving admirer,

Dear Exquisite Mistress,
I hope you are well, in some pleasant endeavor, perhaps a getaway. Your absence reveals my longing for you. Perhaps I got fairly spoiled by your lovely daily letters. In the hollow void of your delayed reply, I am less sure how to

proceed.   I miss you & your firm guidance. I don't want to overload you, as I can write profusely. So, sweet Mistress, I send you this adoring note. As a small service, I note that today makes the 3rd day of your unpaid tribute. I will write occasionally until your light illuminates the proper path. A dark cloudy sky covered the sky of this exotic, mysterious yet utterly enchanting countryside. Night was lasting far more than hours. It had been days with no end in sight. In the deep darkness, with neither moon nor stars for guidance, the pilgrim felt lost & conflicted.   Concern of a mis-step was only part of it. His emotionless intellect offered the possibility of returning. The very unwelcome thought riled him. Besides being difficult to return, he wasn't positive of the way back, especially in the darkness. But that was only his mind... he realized how badly he longed to continue. The decision to continue was easy, he knew it was right as his heart & spirit soared... How to proceed was less easy. At least he still knew the right general direction. He decided to move extremely slowly. Letting his feet feel the way slowly, willing to crawl if need be. It felt good to get a firm feel of the strange land, and to be moving forward, even if slowly

I accidentally sent an unfinished draft of my last letter (then the whole letter). Sorry, so much for fewer letters. In the silence of your absence, I strike a middle ground. I am keeping faith, continuing to tribute you with my words & attention. I am writing alternate days for now, still waiting patiently and hopefully for your reply.

Hello, Goddess, I've missed you!   You are a refreshing and rare find on the internet, and I could feel you changing my mind from when we first spoke. I have this recurring vision of being flooded inside with cum, where everything under my skin is cum, I am cum!

It feels as if I'm swimming in a warm refreshing bath. Perhaps that's why getting fucked over and over again appeals to me so much, it's like squirting cum into a bucket of cum. Thank you for the very hot picture, I wish I were there for you to collar, if I could ever prove myself worthy of such an honor. Will you be available today, Saturday anytime? How much time should I allow for our next call?

Twisted Phone Sex

Mistress Candice

I want to come to you Goddess I know I need your total control and need to be modified in such a way to give you complete access to my life as well as blackmail and total control. However by the time I sign on your gone :(

Mistress, I am ready to worship your breasts. I am still intoxicated from the last time. Now I have cam so you can control me even more. Can call ASAP..............

Like I mentioned earlier, I'm only 5 hours away from you (Victoria, B.C.) I want to set the ALL-TIME RECORD FOR GIVING GODDESS THE MOST ORGASMS SHE HAS EVER EXPERIENCED IN A DAY.

156

You incredible, delightful, all-controlling goddess, you. Thank-you for sending that photo in the E-mail you sent. It is stored securely in the vaults. You are astoundingly beautiful in that photo. Your glamour shots are wonderful, but in this natural shot you transcend the meaning of feminine sexual POWER. It is your most beautiful photo and whenever I think of you I'll think of this photo. That doesn't mean to stop with the glamour stuff, though - I'll always be just as happy to see you with long black gloves, finely latticed "breastplate"-style diamond necklaces, wind blowing through your hair, knee-high boots, slick-with-oil-hooters, expensive, lacy bras and panties........ DAMN I look forward to your personalized "FEEEEED ME" video. I look forward to it more than anything. I am always thinking of myself down on my knees before you and then kissing you, on the pussy, 100 times, as I look into your eyes. 36DD, you say? How bout panties size? Hoping to take that stairway at the foot of my bed to actually see you one day - in the flesh!

Twisted Phone Sex

Mistress Candice

Throughout the day now I get erections at work thinking of getting back home to mindlessly knead the head of my fucking shwagnola as I listen to your "Orgasm" mp3 while looking at your jewelry-bedecked photos, or choking the chicken at your "Feed Me" mp3, which is so beautiful, so perfect you make me think of you a lot more now.........the power of your pussy, its draw, its invincible magnetic power, like a black hole whose gravity is too powerful to resist.........I'm listening SO MUCH to your "Orgasm" mp3, to the extent that I'm memorizing all the peaks and valleys and plateaus that your orgasmic desires take me on a ride for..........a journey I want take again, and again, and again......Your ooooo's and aaaaa's and gasps and inward hisses play themselves out like a symphonic piece of music, replete with crescendoes, and then quitter parts........wonderful. Now if only I could REALLY fuck you.......

In Love, I'm an obedient servant

Beautiful Mistress,

I've had the opportunity to listen to this induction and feel a new-found devotion to You. You are very talented and I was deeply aroused and submissive during the entire session. It seems obvious that You have some professional training in hypnosis. If You have more untested works in the rough, I'd more than happy to give You feedback. ;) As for interests, it turns me on to go blank and lose my mind to a seductive hypno-mistress. Having Your silky words sink deeply into my mind is so lustfully erotic to me. I also love triggers phrases that enforce deep trance and sexual arousal, and do so love orgasm control.

Twisted Phone Sex

Mistress Candice

Lately I've been masturbating about you wickedly putting a prominent lawyer or judge under your erotic hypnotic spell, setting up triggers in him to obey you unconditionally, as you trick him into your trap by telling him to watch very closely and concentrate - as HARD as he can - on the way you put SO MUCH!

oil all over your tits just gushing it on, and then telling him to admire your pretty green eyes, then your lips as you speak to him, and then that wonderful beige stone set in that five-band pearl choker, and then CLOSELY at all the freckles on your chest, and then those luscious, glistening orbs themselves, getting squished, kneaded and brazenly jiggled at your mesmerized victim, loving what he sees, more than anything, his mushy mind becoming more and more receptive to your instructions to admire your beauty.

You slowly, wickedly, convert his admiration into obedience as you goad him further into your snare by challenging him to a "looking at me" contest, telling him how you get your lovers to stare and stare at you for as long as they can, connecting the dots between all your freckles, getting lost in the slow, steady circles your fingertips draw around those nice, stiff, slick nipples, constantly programming your soon-to-be-addicted victim to stare at you longer than ANY OF THE OTHERS, TO WIN THE CONTEST........ Wanting to save up to visit you,

OMMFG!...You mean to tell me that I could get a personalized recording from You?...well, I am a HUGE fan of Your hysterically small recording and vie listened to it many times...I fucking LOVE it!

...especially because it's so creative with the samples added in...LOVE it...if there was the same type of "newer" recording like the $$-dom one or even just a plain old recording of You talking to me, id DIE...I am ALL about small penis humiliation and I flirt with the idea of having to pay for any attention to my tiny/thin cock...if this would interest You, PLEASE let me know...thanks so much!

all Yours,

If only I could just slide my cock so nice and deep inside you and ream you with hard, counter-clockwise gyrations, stretching you out good. If only I could bury my mouth on your pussy with a reverence that would fucking rock your world. If only I could just lick and lick and lick you to your exact specifications.

to jerk off while thinking about you sexually (then, psychologically) manipulating the men in your life by subjecting them to a wicked, evil "CONNECT THE DOTS" contest, prompting them to count as many chest freckles as they possibly fucking can, tell them what "the record" is, and see if they can "surpass" it, in order to attain "Extra Special Satisfaction" from you. As you get them to count out loud, you distract with your soft oooo's and aahhhh's and whisperings like "there's soooooo many of them, aren't there?", "yeah, that's it - keep counting", "I'm not making you lose count am I?" (and then give'em a jiggle) "You're getting lost in them, baby - I can tell". I hope you pussy whip these men for everything they're worth. I hope you so thoroughly seduce - and then ravish (in every possible way imaginable) - the most happily married, most disgustingly richest men out there, and I love to fantasize about all the different modes of seduction you employ to achieve your ends. The only thing I fantasize about more is beef caking you in 14 different positions, while an eight-inch dildo is up your ass, the entire time.

Your lovelorn admirer from Victoria,

This picture just made me cum here at my desk!

Talk to you soon!

YOU know that YOU are the best and the Hottest, and the Sexxxxiest, and the Wildest......and well simply the Bestest......!!!

Those last few photos you sent - they CONTROL my erection, a lot more than maybe almost any other sexy temptress on the internet.....the   photos.....REAFFIRMED matters.

You have to realize, You Seattle Succubus, that this Powerhouse of a Bow-Tie Wearer has appreciated - and gotten off over - thousands upon THOUSANDS of lusciously hot, sexy babes on the internet, women that most normal Joes like us would kill to have simply on a date, and there's probably ten or so maybe that I might return to, a few select group of women who, for the own special reasons, have so enthralled me, impressed me enough to leave a lasting impression.

Twisted Phone Sex

Mistress Candice

The most recent photos you sent hammered home (in the most BRAINWASHINGLY wonderful way) the urgency with which you make this cock-driver gravitate back to you. You are the closest to becoming an addiction. Everything about you is mind-bendingly fucking perfect. You can re-hook and re-hook and re-hook and RE-FUCKING-HOOK my loving testicles, you fucking rewire me, my senses and everything. It's almost like you're coursing through my veins, and I know that if I was ever to actually show you - one on fucking one what universes of yet-to-be-experienced pleasure I could power you into, I would honor what I just said with the balls, heart and soul of a man who could worship you, BETTER THAN ANYONE ELSE.

I am your slave. I also put the slave name you gave me as my user name. This slave will always be loyal to you

166

Now why'd you have to go and send me an invite with free minutes? It took a lot of effort to calm myself down and get back to work and now I'm all excited again. Darn you!

Jesus I feel like I'm almost going out of my fucking mind wondering about things like if there's ever been guys in your life who don't have the means to meet your financial or material desires, but have compensated, quite adequately, in other arenas. I wonder if you crave marathon fuck sessions. I wonder (I might have mentioned this before), if you like boy-girl competitions, whereby the winner can make the other one come first. I wonder TEN TRILLION FUCKING THINGS about you. I could just babble on......

Hi mistress,

I have bought the second brainwash file yesterday ... I love to obey YOU ! I can't wait until I bring myself to submit to you Goddess.

Love

Twisted Phone Sex

Mistress Candice

Why is it every time YOU are here I am NOT......??   :(
Is this all part of your Teasing, Torturing, Tempting,
Tantalizing game of Denial......???   Just how
Loooooooooooooooooonnnnnnnnnnnnnnnnnnnng must
I stay down here on my knees....Begging....?   ;) The
suspense is absolutely KILLIN' ME.......!!!!!
Your ardent admirer,

Just thought I'd send you a note thanking you for
the excellent quality of your downloadable
items...I love the two I've gotten so far...The good
boy trigger (a personal weakness of mine, so I had
to hear it), and your cheerleader video. I'm a big
oral sex fan, and you have the most beautiful, sexy
womanhood I have ever seen, period! And it talks
too! I would love to worship at that shrine until
you drenched my face. Oops, did I say that? How
ungentlemanly...

Thank you dear, you are absolutely lovely, inside
and out

You're Highness

You are so sexy! I beg to kiss Your ass and offer up cash to You as You tongue kiss Your lover...sigh...

Respectfully

Oh Goddess Your stunning beauty is enough to burn me up on the inside and totally weak in the knees... Your voice is way too much to resist... O Goddess it must be so nice to be Your slave and serve Your every command and do whatever You want no matter what. Your slave boy session was way too much for me, I didn't make it till the end... to hot... leaving me as a quivering fool to weak to stand on my feet... I still don't know why they call women the weaker sex... when I see or hear You Goddess I only want to fall to my knees and submit to Your greater power... women are definitely superior to men. No doubt about that. But as to the quality of this mp3... contents... wow.... Sound quality... I know You have Your reasons for it but it's still a shame, I am still convinced that Your beauty deserves perfection and

Twisted Phone Sex Mistress Candice

therefore a higher bitrates to enhance the quality of Your captivating voice. There are many ways of file distribution available on the net which would make this possible... I know You have Your reasons to stick with this but it's still a shame... You are so amazing; I am your devoted servant, forever under your glorious control

Wow... Goddess... You know very well how to make sure resistance is impossible I wish I could speak to You later on but I'm off to work in a minute

Dearest Owner of My manhood,

Those two photos - 22a.jpg and 24.jpg - with the dazzling rays of light reflecting off your jewelry make me want to obey you as I stroke, obey you as I come, obey you as I stroke (Dearest Goddess), obey you as I cum........And those damn freckles! You compelled me, Goddess, to enlarge the photo so I could begin.......... Counting........ As my love for you intensifies, You are perfection my Goddess, thank you so much for the pictures.

Oh my god your legs are... absolutely gorgeous! So sexy and perfect and just simply... incredible! Wow!

Dearest, goddess,

While I'm doing what I can to resist your temptations, making me excel in one-handed typing, I figure I ought to at least acknowledge your gracious offerings as I dare myself to click on each attachment as they 'cum' to me, then click on "open", as the file unveils itself, the tortuously long anticipation obliterated by the joyous, testicle-energizing surprise that you so wickedly 'hook' me with, each and every time, All-Too-Fucking-Perfect Goddess. So, I'll promise to do whatever I can to at least pay you the respect of returning your ALWAYS sweet fucking missives, to detail my reasons to you why each photo you send me has the effect of, well.......making me want to phone you, making me get so helplessly stiff over the crazy rationalization that it's o.k. to go 'deep' into debt over you, because the deeper I go the deeper I am metaphorically fucking you like this fucking stallion will always dream and stroke off and obsess over. The deeper you draw me in the deeper the pleasure will be, the heavier (and of course, the sweeter, the more FUCKING SUPER-CHARGED) the addiction will be, the more attuned to your needs I will be, 'too stiff to say no'. And, of course, the primarily pussy whipped reason for this acknowledgement - your latest photo, (with the effect of another strand or two of soft, soft silk, woven so gently, so seductively.....one "to-die-for" strand at a time, each strand entrapping me further, sucking the soul out of me) is an "angelic" photo, indeed.

Enticing - yes. Inspiring - well, read on.....The look in your eyes makes me stroke just that bit harder - just that right mix of innocence, and dark, ominous, succubus-like magnetism in those eyes. The boobs, the curly locks of blonde hair, the funky, enhanced color of the background, that reddish-pink shade of nail polish. It's good for my cock! The previous email I sent - I could kick myself for forgetting to mention how - when I zoomed in several times - the glittering necklace helped guide me to your freckles, compelling me to count and stroke, repeatedly.....lovingly.

Entrapped......

Twisted Phone Sex Mistress Candice

OMG you're absolutely stunning. Just... beyond gorgeous. It's mind boggling to see how perfect you are, to listen to your mp3's and hear how incredible your voice is. You are simply gorgeous and so beautiful and... Just, wow! It easy to fall into the fantasy of being nothing but your bitch, used and abused and living every day to worship you for as perfect and powerful as you are.

I can only hope that you so thoroughly pussy whipped the shit out of the owner of the yacht. And if there were deckhands, I'm almost praying that you gave them the bluest fucking balls they've ever had, so that when you snapped your fingers it was fucking impossible for them to try resisting from sneaking off with you to get their cock and balls owned.

174

You have the nicest fucking tits. Period. I love them. Oh to just fuck and fuck and fuck you on the deck of that boat, banging you, with the sea breeze and rolling swells. If you fell off - you'd have to become a mermaid! Thank-you, again, for the photo.

Your voice is so good I just want to listen and please I think I would do anything you said. I think it is so cool how you can make someone cum on command and how you can make them cum with out touching themselves. I hope to talk to you later Thanks for keeping things in order and not fucking with me I am not sure How crazy I could be. Later I hope

Twisted Phone Sex Mistress Candice

I love you.

I think I honest to god fucking, fucking, FUCKING love you. I love how you eventually ensnare me once again. A game of cat and mouse that becomes so arousing it is treacherously addictive. I love, more than anything, what you do to me. My nightly prayer, lately, has been that you start to get, like, REALLY FUCKING GOOD at learning to hypnotize, so that you're eventually able to sexually distract your victims, whether you're flirting, or fucking the soul out of them, as you wickedly let the light reflect off your crystal pendant and into their increasingly receptive eyes. I fantasize about you doing corporate espionage, whereby you're hired by your target firm as a therapist, and then you have one-on-one sessions with the senior employees who have access to information, that, in the wrong hands, could spell ruin for the company. After they've all become your mindless fuck-zombies, you make a couple million dollars, selling that info to the "wrong hands". I can tell your hypnotic powers are evident in other areas, like your sperm-generating mp3's, or when you describe your seductive prowess at cock teasing when you strip, creating the overwhelming illusion of the PROMISE of sexual release, only to enrapture, to manipulate, and to "cajole the old' cock for cash" trick.   And speaking of cajoling cocks for cash, (wow! the alliteration!) I tried so....fucking... hard to resist tributing you for your birthday last Friday, and I thought I'd made it through, and then you end up doing it to me, anyway, with the "look deep" photo you just sent. Believe you me, I looked deep, alright, and STILL managed to hold back from ejaculating as I went through the delicious click, click, click steps of getting a tribute to you. Dieing to cum, but also dieing for more of your pleasure,

Twisted Phone Sex

Mistress Candice

Mistress all I can do is think of You. I now know that I belong to You forever and I long for You and need You. I have no defenses against You and don't want any. I am so grateful You spend time with me and I want to please You by doing anything I can for You. I can still see Your perfect breasts and smell Your essence and want them to stay with me forever. I know I am powerless and I know You will take everything I have and I only hope I can live up to Your standards. I will try very hard to make You happy. please let me know what I can do to make You happy and I can't wait for the succubus to return. once again I am Yours completely Mistress Candace

Thank you for the pictures. Don't you feel a little ashamed of yourself, constantly teasing a weak-willed boy who gets a boner every time he sees your pictures, and can't get thoughts of our previous conversations out of his head?

Mistress;

Your pictures are amazing and your invitation to chat is appealing; however I have a jealous wife and a pre-nup that guaranties I won't ever talk to anyone on NF or Keen. Sorry. I did pick up one of your programs out of curiosity and that was bad enough. I listened to it a couple of times and it got to where I really wanted to talk to you. I felt myself becoming more and more involved; I erased it. The feelings were nice but the problems way too hazardous to my health to pursue it. Thanks

Dear Mistress,

I feel the need to tell You that I am completely devoted to You, Goddess. It is as if You have been the missing value to my life and now that I am Yours I feel complete. You are a real Goddess to be worshipped and pleased.

Wow that training program really goes deep I just can't stop listening to Your voice, I just have to hear it at least once a day... every day. highly. very HIGHLY addictiveand oh

Twisted Phone Sex

Mistress Candice

god You are so stunning beautiful and Your eyes Mistress...
WoW... are they really that green? I'm in love I'm in love I'm
in love I'm in love I'm in love I'm in trouble

just heavenly addicted,

How are you doing? Hope you are doing well. Where can I get pictures from your website? Especially the casual ones? You look very beautiful in those!!! Well you look GREAT!!! in all of them. But those caught my eye, because they are very natural. Take Care, Hugs

I love YOUR "hypnosis pictures" (with a pendulum or just YOUR eyes). pictures on which YOUR are dressed like a witch casting a spell or like a queen must be fantastic too (just one fantasy about YOU). ok, I must get back to study for university ... I will try not to think about YOU ! have a hypnotic day and a good hunt for new pets

Dearest Goddess let me again tell you what a wonderful time I had under your hypnotic spell. I have been hypnotized many times but these last two times with you just drove me out of my mind. Your hypnotic voice weaving a magical trip into your world combined with those extremely hypnotic green eyes are impossible to resist, Of course I don't want to. It is now five hours after my trip to heaven and I think I am just coming out of your hypnotic power, Of course I see your face everywhere and my world is better for it. Your hypnotic voice is in my head and those divesting green eyes are etched into my brain. Everywhere I look I see you're those magical eyes and start to drift off into your wonderful land of hypnotic bliss. Your beautiful green are to powerful for us mortal men and I certainly hope you wear sun glasses when you are outside to keep the whole world from falling at your feet. Of course there is still that lovely voice that works into your brain and makes you want to obey it without even knowing why. Your overwhelming hypnotic power had my head seeing you but my body was totally lost in your hypnotic world. It was to devastating to believe. The next time I hope to be able to spend even more time under your wonderful entrancing power. One word from you and I grow weak and want to live in your hypnotic world. You can throw away that pocket watch you have on your web site no one can resist those hypnotic blue eyes. Add that to that sweet voice from heaven and you can take over the world one slave at a time

I am in trance now I masturbated three times today I need to prove my devotion oh dear oh dear ooooooohhh god this is sooo incredible HOT I wish I could kneel behind You and touch it and kiss it and worship it jeezzz this makes me feel so totally aroused oh boy I'm afraid I'm a ass worshipper. You are just sooo stunning beautiful in every way I eh... wow... this has something to do with the last session I just listen to hasn't it. OOh.. Goddess You are soooooooooooo devious... dangerous... but also heaven all the way.

Twisted Phone Sex

Mistress, I am your boy toy I am your whore, here to make you money and serve you, total submitted to you and at your feet. I love when you put your leash and collar on me Wow !! Those written words sent such a sexual jolt thru my body. You have the keys in Your possession. You now confirm what I have know for many months, You do control me and I do belong to You, Mistress

Twisted Phone Sex Mistress Candice

I am so sorry to have been away for so long from You, it has been agony for me. On Feb 29th, I was driving back from the adult bookstore, having visited the glory hole and on the way back I was in a car crash. A drunk driver crossed the center line and hit squarely in the left front of my car. Fortunately the airbags did there job, but I suffered a broken ankle, left arm, rib, and collar bone. When they took me to the emergency room they had to cut the padlock off the CB3000 , although I begged them not to. I wasn't even ashamed having it on; in fact I wanted it to remain on until I could get back to You. I was in the hospital for two days and then stayed at my sister and brother-in-laws until this morning since I could walk around very easily. Anyway, I have ordered another CB3000 and lock which should be here Monday. The worst part of it all, worse than my car being ruined and worse than not being able

to work, was not being with You. I realized how empty my life is without Your control and how much I need to serve You . It is so good to see Your pictures again and to hear Your voice on the mp3s, but I won't feel normal until I am kneeling and listening to Your sweet voice live again. I miss You so very much and absolutely worship everything about You . I belong to You and always will.

Your obedient slave

Goddess, I am missing you so I hope you are around soon last time you stood me up and I have not recovered, Need to become your mindless slave for eternity. DO what ever you see fit with me. Everything I have is yours, my mind, body, and soul all my belongings are yours

Twisted Phone Sex

Mistress Candice

Goddess, you are foremost in my thoughts! I find myself stroking my chastity device while thinking of you. My pain is unimportant knowing it brings you pleasure. I am so proud that you hold the keys to my cb6000. My love for you grows daily. I need you!

Chapter Six
General Requests
and Comments

If I were to include every E-mail ever received from my clients, this would be the largest chapter by far. It would also be the most boring and redundant. Not all requests were legal, wanted or received a response. Some are funnier than others, but I believe this chapter shows just how diverse and creative fantasies can get. This last chapter rounds out earlier chapters to show a good representation of what a woman in the phone sex industry is likely to see.

Do you make lots of noise when you have sex? I like girls to be realllllllllllllllll loud screaming loud in fact. Is that doable?

I am feeling extra horny and sort of daring myself to try a call with you again. Maybe best not to play with fire but I was able to stop after our previous call, so maybe I am strong enough to not worry about you. Anyway, hope you have a nice day.

Can you pretend you're my naughty neighbor coming over to seduce me but pretending you are looking for my wife?

I need to call you today!! Need to watch your video again while we talk. The site accidentally deleted all my mail and I had to start as a new profile. Can you send me the link again? Thanks sweetie...

I want to watch my hot wife getting fucked hard!! Will call you ASAP!!!

When are you going to be available, I think your so beautiful and the sexiest women on earth

Twisted Phone Sex   Mistress Candice

Would you put on a show for me and my wife? She likes women too but she is a little shy so she won't let me turn on our cam. Do you mind?

You look like an amazing mistress in your pictures

I am a novice and need training but do you use hypnosis?

Twisted Phone Sex

Mistress,

Can you pretend you're my next door neighbor who has the hot's for me. You saw my wife leave for a trip and now you want to come over and seduce me. I fight and say no no no but I finally give in when you start playing with your pussy and force me to have sex with you.

Are you Bi? I love women and would love to watch you. Have you ever done a show for a woman before?

May I worship you on cam...Goddess?

Twisted Phone Sex

Are you on cam now Ma'am? I cannot talk on the phone but I would like cam and chat if possible. Thank you

Hi,

I would like to call you again soon and have you watch me on cam. Just not in the best mood today.

You are giving me blue balls by not being available on cam. Please let me know when you will be on cam again.

Thanks,

Have you cum yet today?

I would love to role play with you. I would like you in a sexy secretary outfit willing to do anything to me as your boss to get a raise.

I am dying to talk to you again. Everything you did to me worked so well, it's terrifying. But I can't quite seem to get away, or to get the time to call you in private. In my desperation, I've had a crazy idea. Do you think there's any chance I could pay you to create mp3 recordings for me? I've got a 30 minute train ride to and from NYC every day. It would be amazing if I could listen to recordings on the way to and from work. Hammer home all your suggestions. Obviously not force me to act, while on the train, but would drive me insane nonetheless. The only time I seem to be able to get any quiet these days, is really early in the morning. It's awful! I am going nuts. I need to hear you so bad!!!

PS-- In the last two weeks, amazing things have happened. Talking to you is like a magic spell... was completely life altering. Now I'm just dying to hear you so bad, it aches...

What do you think?

Twisted Phone Sex

Mistress Candice

Hi Can hypnosis help me get over someone/ failed relationship quicker?? Can/ will you do this or do you know of any one who will??? I have been DYING to see you. This is what we did to me last time, in case you don't remember me. :(It's been horrible without you. Please please drop me a line if you're up for doing this again, taking me even deeper. Making it even more powerful....

A husband finally gets a well-deserved half day of work, and gets home hours before his wife, only to meet the new babysitter for the first time....... She's young, cute, and dressed pretty skimpy. After introductions, I offer to give you some money, so you can be on your way........ But, you pretend you were hoping you could stay the full shift until the wife gets home because you really need the money. Truth of the matter is you have the hots for the man you just met and at first try to send subtle hints, until sexual frustration sets in and do more than hint around... you flash, tease, talk dirty, and even promise not to tell my wife if you can just have some of that cock right now!! Does this sound like fun???

Twisted Phone Sex

Mistress Candice

Can you be a sexy college co ed and pretend I'm your professor. You need a better grade so you come into my office and sit on my desk. I ignore you and keep working so you spread your legs slowly, getting my attention until I can't stand it any more and bury my head in your crotch. Then you turn the tables on me and make me plow you from behind. What do you think?

Hey, I saw you're on tonight, and I do want to play. I just got home from work, so I need to clean up and prepare, hopefully you'll be on for at least 15 more minutes. I will try to call you tonight when you get free. You look busy right now. I sent this to make it easy to find what we did last time (I know I called last night, was just trying to make it as easy for you as possible). Hope its ok that I'm dying to hear you again so soon.

Do you dress as a sexy secretary? I would like for you to do anything to get a raise and keep your job

Twisted Phone Sex

Just wondering if you have sheer pantyhose available for cam today.... Let me know...

Hey babe, I am looking for a hot chick to smoke, wear a corset, or girl on girl. Can you help me with any of these? I will pay the money, but I am trying to find a chick that can satisfy at least one of these.

God, i have checked so many times and not found you in, and then I found you just now. By time I got to pressing button to dial, you were busy. Then went from busy to alerts-on. I am just not succeeding.

Twisted Phone Sex Mistress Candice

Good afternoon Goddess was just thinking of you. I was thinking have You ever thought to make mp3's or record Your own CD's, or even DVD's for training Your slaves?

Mistress, what will you do to me when I call? I am new to the submissive role, and want to learn. Also, I have a cam I can set up so you can watch me do what you say. Please give me a list of item I will need to have handy when I call you. Thank you Mistress.

I need my balls drained soon...can you help?

Hey there Hun, let me first just say you are absolutely the most beautiful girl on this site, hands down. What outfit do you have on today? And also do you like to watch as well? Thanks Hun,

Twisted Phone Sex

Fuck I need to "cum" see you, badly.........Is there a main man in your life right now?

I know I have said this before and I am not saying I would do it all right now but if I pay my debt may I still be your little toy? Please let me know

Hello I have been interested in conversing with you for a while, but never seem to find a time that you and I are online simultaneously. I had thought maybe for awhile that you don't get out here anymore, but then saw that you've got recent feedback. Please advise and inform me. Thank you very much

Twisted Phone Sex Mistress Candice

I find it very difficult to reach you on here. I loved our call and I notice you post a notice when you are on but I am never home. When you are on you are always busy. I guess that's why they say you are the best. Anyway I would love to know if you have a schedule or a time that I know will fit with mine. I would love to hear back from you.

I was wondering if you could do a POV foot tickling torture clip where it looks like the watcher is tickling your feet hysterically while ankles and wrists tied up? If yes, how much would you charge for say a few minutes of that?

Are you ready for an internet cam slut with little dick for you on Sunday or Monday?

Hey baby, I am 21.m...can we just fuck on the phone or do I have to be into that cuckold

Hello,

Do you do custom videos? Where you are dominant?

Are you showing off legs today?

Can you be my wife?

I so want to play with you... you know how beautiful I think you are... and when are you coming to visit me in London?

Twisted Phone Sex

Hey babe, want to tease me tonight?? If so what would you wear out to the club to tease the hell out of me??

Marry me please

You have outstanding breasts! They would look perfect wrapped around my c..k

Hi, I was wondering if you have someone who could tickle your feet while I listen? If so, how much time would you need to arrange it? I'm in California.

Hi, do you have long nails now? I have a very strong long nail fetish, the sound of them tapping or clicking is controlling to me

Hey there hot stuff. Might be able to call you shortly for an "explosive" time

You are so beautiful. I'd love to cum with or for, or on you.

I wish I was there to eat some sweet pussy

Twisted Phone Sex Mistress Candice

Thank you for sending your Pictures on to me also. Forgive me on that last call, I am at my Fathers place and I rarely get here as I live out west and the neighbor girls seen me out in the back yard and wanted to say Hello. It was a little awkward to continue with our call. I've not really done anything through this site before, I have used my web cam though also I am on Eastern Standard Time now so I would guess You're on mountain time like me when in alberta. 2 hours later then eastern time? and so what time will You do Your show?

Sorry I missed your shift I need you , please email me when I may call, you're pet ,

Would really like a visual to help me produce my offerings to you...:) can you turn your cam on?

I would so love to meet u for a session that ended up me having to eat your cream pie... u rock...

Hi:

I sure wish I could cum over and play with you tonight but I have some friends coming by this month and they are fundamentalist Christians. You know, the ones who leave out the "fun" :-(. Anyway I'll try to come back in October.

Hi, I am going to call you exactly at 11:04. I cannot really talk on the phone so know that it is me if I whisper!

Twisted Phone Sex
Mistress Candice

I have a thing for sex-bots. Can you talk and move like you are a sex android and you are a refurbished model for rent. They rent you out because you have this glitch that every time you say a dirty word you keep repeating it. When I touch your nipples you give off a special lubricant to make you wet and when I have you touch your belly button you cum. But I want you to talk like a robot and move like one too. Can you do that?

Hi, its 7:40am and I have just a few minutes before I need to go to airport, was wondering if you could force out my last come before I leave, the power if you need would have me so hooked, please be mean and force me to release all my hot come,

What color are your nails painted?

It's been forever since we've had one of our typed out role-plays over the phone... so I want to leave you with this extra teasing one for the next time you're online... Hope to hear from you soon... I miss the diverse voice of your's...

Hi, I have to leave in a bit, I was wondering if you could empty out all my hot stuff from my balls, begging.

Your tease and denial file got me again. but I can't really talk because of my neighbors Can I call you and hear your instructions? I have ear piece so I can be able to hear you very well. hope you reply me soon

Twisted Phone Sex Mistress Candice

I love your profile. Are we able to view each other over webcam while we talk on the phone? I have a web cam. Thank You Mistress,

Would you dance seductively for me like you are at a club and then get on your knees and pretend you're sucking my dick?

Can you pretend to be my teacher and spank me with a ruler?

I can't play now but I want to schedule an appointment for next week while I'm at work. Do you schedule that far in advance?

Hi. I'm looking for a woman to be a part of a very realistic sort of office roleplay. She would be my boss and I her underling. The office is a travel agency. She will pop into my

208

office at her convenience and give me assignments, telling me to find flight and hotel info for various cities, and then she will also pop in and get my reports. To facilitate this working relationship on NF, I will have my messenger on at all times while I'm at work, and she can IM me at any time and have me call her. She can also send me on errands or other assignments as she sees fit. If interested in this, you would be paid for all the phone/cam time of course, but you could also charge me on top of this, maybe a small fee per each assignment. My interest in all of this is one of a real life sort of set up of control. I work alone most of the time in real life and long for a realistic sort of relationship with a female boss. The time in this would not be overly extensive, maybe an average of 15 minutes a day, and you could just be yourself. Let me know if interested. Thanks -

Up until very recently I've been emailing round flirts asking who can make a nasty giantess voice file, which some nice results. However your sexy profile and cam is inspiring me to risk asking for more. Namely a nasty horny giantess vid. Would you be comfortable with the twisted giantess tale, where our heroine teases and punishes (fatally), helpless, naked, turned on and terrified little men? All you'd need is a toy soldier (or some similar male figure preferably about 2cm high), and rather than describing him struggling between your awesome breasts, or being swallowed whole, or inserted in your ravenous pussy, you could show me! With the accompanying sound of your teasing, desciptions and happy noises! Unbelievably, prick drippingly hot (if you're a twisted old perve like me :-) Is this something you'd

Twisted Phone Sex

be willing to make for me? Whatever your answer. I wish you well.

Disclaimer, in case you're worried, I'm not in the real world a sicko psycho. Outside of here I would'nt hurt a fly.

Hi, can you handle a role play like this? Let me know and I will call asap.... your my wife's older sister in from out of town for business. she is busy today so we make plans to have dinner. I come by your hotel to pick you up and you suggest eating in given that you have a terrific suite. You and I have always enjoyed each other's company and today is no different. We settle in on the couch, chat, laugh, etc. We are sitting right next to each other and you make sure we have constant contact..your hand on my knee, your stocking clad leg abuts mine...you want to know if you can ask me a serious question...something on your mind.....you light a cigarette....you ask how yoru body compares to your sisters? you then ask me to closely examine diff parts of your body including your legs which you say you always thought were far better....you are wearing a business outfit so you ask me to remove your stockings so I can get a closer look and feel...you can tell I am getting weaker and weaker so you come next to me and whsiper in my ear so that your perfume surrounds me...you ask me if I think I married the wrong sister...I try to say no but you slide me inside you and tell me that you are in complete control of me now..that I must now always think of you when I make love to my wife...let me know if you are game and can pull this off. happy for you to modify.

Thanks!! I find the idea so hot - imagine me listening to your voice every nighy, madly jerking my tiny cock and coming again and again, knowing all the while that I'm setting myself up for a massive humiliation with Kathy. Knowing that each cum makes it that much less likely I'll ever please a woman again. Practicing, if you will, for the main event ;) Anyways, I'll be happy with whatever you come up with.

Hi,

Twisted Phone Sex

Mistress Candice

I know this might sound a little weird but if you like it just email me back. I like to role-play you are a sex android. I want you to move and talks like a robot but your skin is synthetic and feels like real skin. Your nipples are like buttons and if I touch your right one it makes your pussy lubricate and if I touch your left one it makes you beg for cock. If I stick my finger in your belly button it makes you cum. Your pussy is refurbished and built to fit my dick. You are programmed to want me and talk to dirty to me to get me to fuck you. Interested?

Twisted Phone Sex

Last night I went to a concert. I met a guy and his girlfriend there waiting for it to start. Her name was Roxanne. They were really friendly. Anyway. On the way back to the bathroom, she pulled me aside, pressed me up against the wall and said "You better kiss me now or you are going to regret it!" So I did. Kissed her hard, long, deep. The whole concert her boyfriend had his arms around her but she kept flirting with me all night. Later when her bf went for drinks for us she put her hand around the back of my head, fingers through my hair and pulled me down t other for a long, wet, deep kiss. She grabbed my hand and pulled it around to squeeze her ass. Then she started kissing my ear (which drives me CRAZY) and begged me to sneak her back to the hotel before her bf got back and fuck the total shit out of her. I waited about 2 seconds too long to act and her bf came back. Damn it!! Can you help me play this out?

Twisted Phone Sex

Hello I love your profile and I think you are exactly what I am looking for on here. My fantasy has always been being seduced by my mother's friend, and you have a lot of similarities to her. If you have any interest in fulfilling my fantasy, then please email me back. Thanks

Looking for some milf neighbor role play. If you could like narrate something for me as i watch you . Looking for cleavage tease and you bent over doggy with thong on let me know thanks.

Do u have a school uniform?

Hi Mistress,

I am going outside to tan in my bikinni right now and then I have to go to the store in about an hour or so to buy some new sandals. May I call you from the store and have you on speaker as you call me out loudly as a being a whore, slut and whatever else you can think to call me. Also, if you want *me to make other purchases, you can guide me through them on the phone. I will check my email before I go to see if I may call you\ Goddess, I am soooo horny today and I can't stop thinking about you. The chastity device has been very tight since we spoke. I want it removed, but not nearly as much as I want to please you! I keep looking at the picture of your ass. My desire to worship it is overwhelming. What would I do just to have my lips feel your toes and ass? I would love just to have my lips touch your panties knowing they were once against you. Sorry, I'm rambling OMG! Hot! Damn! You look amazing in this pic, and Your legs... omg Your legs are gorgeous! Every inch of You is perfect, I'm a leg guy and my jaw hit the floor when i saw this pic... damn!*

Twisted Phone Sex

Mistress Candice

Biography
of Miss Candice

The day finally arrived where I was no longer a child and was required to make a choice as to what to do with my life. The only thing I knew for certain was college was not an option. I wasn't a good student and rebelled against authority just for the sake of rebelling. I knew myself well enough to know that wasn't about to change. After working a vast array of menial jobs from janitorial work to waitress in a fine dining establishment, I eventually found a tolerable profession answering phones.

Working my way up from receptionist to bookkeeper to office manager by the time I was 22, it was abundantly clear this was a dead end job in a dead end field. Regardless of the various titles they bestowed upon me and the minuscule raises given, I was reminded daily, no matter how subtle, that I was the lowest of the low on the white collar totem pole.

My meager salary only slightly above minimum wage, I was guaranteed, based on performance, to receive an annual raise. Unfortunately the increase in pay didn't always match the increase in the annual cost of living. I worked with women older than I in similar positions with college degrees and their pay was not much more than mine. Yet most were content and even happy. Still paying off college loans, some were married and subjugating the family income, their pay just extra money. Others struggled working second jobs or juggling kid's schedules yet they still seemed to find a second home in their personally decorated cubicles.

To me, a young single woman trying to find her way, the prospect of walking down that path was not about living life it was about barely surviving it. I was determined, for me, it would be nothing more than a stepping stone to stand on while I decided where I wanted to go.

Unable to make ends meet while contemplating what to do with the rest of my life, I decided to do what the other girls in my position did: take a second job. I saw an ad in the paper for a cocktail waitress. Something I could do; something I had done before. At the time I didn't realize the position was in a topless bar. Completely ignorant to their very existence, I was only slightly surprised when I walked through those doors for the first time. I was without preconceived ideas, notions or prejudices; to me it was just another place, another job, another option, additional income. The manager was kind and reassuring, my uniform was a bathing suit not my birthday suit.

He promised there was more money to be made in his club then any generic night club, and he was right. Not only did I make more money I had more fun. It was only a matter of time before one tiny slight by my ego bloated boss gave me the excuse needed to justify quitting my whipping

Twisted Phone Sex

boy position and waitressing full-time. Of course that didn't last long once I heard the dancers exaggerate their nightly earnings! The transition from waitress to dancer was as natural and smooth as the silk thongs we wore.

At first I didn't have a plan other than to sock away as much money as I could while I could. Then opportunities began to present themselves. Invited to join a competition for a calendar contest led to an overabundance of small time modeling jobs, of which I eagerly accepted. Calendars, magazines, posters, a music video, ring girl and I even toured the country with a dance troupe. By the time I realized this was not the path to becoming a super model, it didn't matter anymore. I found myself deep in a relationship and pregnant.

Once married and raising a child, I made the mistake many women do to their own detriment, stripper or not. I agreed to work and put my husband through college in exchange; once he was employable, he would do the same for me. As is common in this age-old story he didn't hold up his end of the deal. Six years later, I became a single parent without the skills necessary to get a "straight" job that paid well enough to raise my daughter supervised. So I continued dancing while being both mother and father to a troubled child who had been abandoned by her father, physically, emotionally and financially. Even with supportive parents who helped more than I like to admit, our efforts to recover from the annihilation of a life plan was more than a simple set back.

Well aware that exotic dancing was not a permanent solution, as youth is prized and I wasn't getting younger, coupled with my daughter's changing needs as she grew older, it was once again time to find new options. I had sacrificed nine years of having a social life to manage my heavily burdened schedule. Already stretched to my limits I knew that if I didn't find another way, another plan, we would be thrown back into crisis. Juggling became the new trick, always one ball in the air as I navigated through the sea of possibilities. Trying one business after the next while maintaining a full time position in the entertainment industry, I was ready too try almost anything. I owned a mail box store, I became a certified massage therapist, I went to Real Estate school, I even became a book dealer. Each and every position failed to live up to its promise and our needs, for a variety of reasons.

My options becoming fewer by the day, I refused to give up hope. It was critical I adjust. Finally, a friend of mine shared what she had been keeping secret for months: this great new thing called "web-camming." All that was required was a computer and a web cam. I had both. No start up costs, no overhead, work from home at my convenience, sounded perfect especially as there was nothing to lose.

Introduced to one site, I discovered there were countless choices. As with stripping, I decided to work for the most reputable. Eventually, I ended up on two sites. One site was cam only and one site you had the option of cam and phone or just phone. The internet porn industry accommodates everyone. No matter how old you are, how much you weigh or what your interests are there is a place for you. Unless you are doing cam you don't even need real photos of yourself. More phone sex operators than not go to content web sites and buy pictures of women they portray as themselves to their customers.

After a couple years of "web-camming" and "phone sex," I discovered an entire community dedicated to Erotic Hypnosis. I had been using hypnosis for insomnia for over a decade and became a certified hypnotist. Utilizing my skills in hypnosis with my own personal sexual experience, I knew I had a product for an existing market. Elated at the prospect of broadening my customer base I added "Hypno-Dom" to my listings and almost over night it became the most popular form of entertainment I offer.

Throughout the 23 years of working in the personal entertainment industry, I have spoken with literally thousands of men. Through them I have learned more about human nature then I ever thought possible, including my own. The one-on-one exchange I have practiced is so personal in nature it often allows insight into the human psyche that other jobs cannot match. It's a given my customers the chance to share their deepest, darkest desires, fantasies and secrets. But to my astonishment, they also share the most mundane details of their lives, for which I'm grateful. I have no doubt its easier to anonymously share a kinky fantasy than it is to share the details of their interpersonal relationships with their wives, kids and jobs. I find it most rewarding when they confess their dreams of what could have been and what they hope will be, sharing that last inch they usually reserve and hide for themselves, unshared with those closest to them they give to me freely.

My job has been more than just a job it is an intimate experience which has contributed far greater benefits than adding to my bank account. I have been given a glimpse into the fantasies of men and beyond. Invited into places where no one else has gone. Through this I have learned, in spite of a wide variety of sexual proclivities, we are all very much alike, we all long for total acceptance. In one form or another we need a break from our own reality no matter how happy we are in that reality and at some point we will seek total acceptance for what we perceive to be the worst of ourselves even if it's from a complete stranger. My customers not only share their deepest, darkest desires, fantasies and secrets but to my astonishment, they also share the most mundane details of their lives, for which I'm grateful.

Life is a series of stepping stones; stability does not exist, it is an illusion. Life is a constant state of change. To remain rigid, unyielding, intolerant and unchanging only brings about misery. In adapting to life's changes and being true to myself in the process I have found happiness in my choices. I live my life; I do not simply exist.

Twisted Phone Sex

Mistress Candice

www.ingramcontent.com/pod-product-compliance
Lightning Source LLC
Chambersburg PA
CBHW021225090426
42740CB00006B/378